THE MERCHANT OF VENICE

THE MERCHANT OF VENICE

William Shakespeare

Edited by
CEDRIC WATTS

WORDSWORTH CLASSICS

First published in 2000 by Wordsworth Editions Limited
Cumberland House, Crib Street, Ware, Hertfordshire SG12 9ET

ISBN I 84022 431 2

Typeset by Antony Gray
Printed and bound in Great Britain by
Mackays of Chatham plc, Chatham, Kent

CONTENTS

GENERAL INTRODUCTION

The Wordsworth Classics' Shakespeare Series, with *Henry V* as its inaugural volume, presents a newly-edited sequence of William Shakespeare's works. Wordsworth Classics are inexpensive paperbacks for students and for the general reader. Each play in the Shakespeare Series is accompanied by a standard apparatus, including an introduction, explanatory notes and a glossary. The textual editing takes account of recent scholarship while giving the material a careful reappraisal. The apparatus is, however, concise rather than elaborate. We hope that the resultant volumes prove to be handy, reliable and helpful. Above all, we hope that, from Shakespeare's works, readers will derive pleasure, wisdom, provocation, challenges, and insights: insights into his culture and ours, and into the era of civilisation to which his writings have made – and continue to make – such potently influential contributions. Shakespeare's eloquence will, undoubtedly, re-echo 'in states unborn and accents yet unknown'.

CEDRIC WATTS
Series Editor

INTRODUCTION

I

In the law-court scene towards the end of *The Merchant of Venice*, Shylock thinks he is winning and can thrust his knife into Antonio, but the process suddenly turns against him, and he is thoroughly vanquished. The history of Shakespeare's *The Merchant of Venice* indicates that though it seems to invite condemnation as an anti-Semitic text, it has repeatedly, in performance, revealed a contrasting nature. Shylock, though vanquished in the law-court, triumphs in the theatre: a character so intense that he dominates the play and threatens to render frivolous the romantic intrigues at Belmont.

Of course, the evidence for treating *The Merchant of Venice* as a perniciously anti-Semitic work is clear.[1] A perennial anti-Semitic stereotype depicts Jews as usurious, cunning, malevolent and potentially or actually murderous. It's a stereotype which extends from mediæval times to the present. In Chaucer's 'Prioress's Tale', Jews of Lincoln are depicted as ruthless murderers of young Hugh, the innocent choir-boy; in Marlowe's *The Jew of Malta*, Barabas is avaricious, callous and Machiavellian; in Ezra Pound's *Cantos*, Jews are reviled as the usurious foes of civilised order. In various parts of the world, and among various political groups, the 'demonisation' of Jews continues.

Historically, Shakespeare's characterisation of Shylock has certainly featured in international anti-Semitic propaganda. Surveying the play's influence, John Gross notes that, in 1832, a Tasmanian newspaper denounced Jewish immigrants as 'Shylocks' and 'incubuses'; in 1882, a writer in the *New York Times* warned its readers against sympathising with the victims of pogroms in Russia, for those people showed that 'Shylock was not the mere creation of a poet's fancy'; in 1894, the Melbourne *Age* declared that 'the Hebrew . . . is and must remain the Shylock of the nations'; and, in 1920, an Englishman, E. S. Spencer, published *Democracy or Shylocracy?*, which he described as 'a graphic exposure of Jew corruption in Finance, Politics and Society'.[2] In *Shakespeare and Elizabethan Poetry* (1951), M. C. Bradbrook, a distinguished literary critic at Cambridge University, curiously remarked: 'The concentration camps of Nazi Germany bred many heroes and martyrs but also a few Shylocks.'[3]

In that Nazi Germany, *The Merchant of Venice* was frequently staged: there were thirty productions between 1934 and 1939, for instance. When it was staged in Berlin in 1942, the director, Paul Rose, distributed actors among the audience, so that when Shylock appeared in the trial scene, 'the voice of the people chimed in from the gallery, their angry cries and shrill whistles echoed from the stalls'. In Vienna, in May 1943, *The Merchant of Venice* was performed by command of the Nazi Gauleiter, Baldur von Schirach, who had publicly declared that

> every Jew active in Europe is a danger to European culture. If people want to criticise me for deporting tens of thousands of Jews from this city . . . I can only answer that I see it as a positive contribution to European culture.

Approximately nine million Jews lived in the European countries conquered by the Nazis. Six million of them were systematically murdered. Von Schirach was a zealous accomplice.[4]

The title-page of the First Quarto of *The Merchant of Venice* refers to the 'extreame crueltie' of Shylock. That cruelty is one of the blatant features of the play. He is murderous as well as usurious and anti-Christian. He makes his motives clear from the outset, when he says of Antonio:

> I hate him for he is a Christian;
> But more, for that in low simplicity
> He lends out money gratis, and brings down
> The rate of usance here with us in Venice.
> If I can catch him once upon the hip,
> I will feed fat the ancient grudge I bear him.

Shylock is cunning, mercenary, ruthless, implacable – and a Jew.

Repeatedly the play demonises Jewish people generally by depicting Shylock as a representative (albeit extreme) of his race. In the earliest texts, his speech-heading is sometimes 'Shylocke', 'Shy.' or 'Shyl.', and sometimes 'Jew' (spelt 'Iew' or 'Iewe'). The Christians – including even Portia in her 'quality of mercy' speech – repeatedly address him as 'Jew' or 'the Jew'. He is likened to a dog, a wolf, and even Satan. 'Certainly the Jew is the very devil incarnation', says Lancelet Gobbo. (Lancelet is 'famished in the Jew's service', while Shylock will accept a dinner-invitation from those he detests: 'I'll go in hate, to feed upon / The prodigal Christian'). Solanio describes Shylock as 'the devil . . . in the likeness of a Jew'; to Bassanio he is 'the cruel devil'. Even Jessica, his daughter, says 'Our house is hell', and seizes with alacrity the opportunity to elope with a Christian.

The contrasts could not be more systematic, it appears. Shylock is usurious and seeks to slice a Christian's flesh, whereas Antonio, the Christian merchant, makes interest-free loans, rescues Shylock's victims and risks his life to provide funds for a friend. Shylock is grasping and calculative; the Christians are venturesome, romantic speculators: Antonio sends forth his laden ships, Bassanio ventures to win Portia. The Jew is associated with hatred and cruelty, the Christians with love and mercy. In contrast to Shylock's preoccupation with usury, with the bond and the letter of the law, there lies the romantic world of Belmont, where the bonds that matter are bonds of love; and beyond the grating discords of Shylock's vindictiveness sounds Belmont's sweet music, the harmonies that link lovers to each other and to the starry heavens above.

Shakespeare was as uninhibited in borrowing from previous writers as Bassanio was in borrowing from Antonio. One likely source of *The Merchant of Venice* is Giovanni Fiorentino's collection of tales, *Il pecorone*, written at the end of the sixteenth century. This includes the story of Giannetto and the rich lady of Belmonte. To pursue his courtship of the lady, Giannetto becomes indebted to his friend Ansaldo, a Venetian merchant who borrows money from a cunning Jew. Giannetto wins the lady but forgets his friend's plight. When Ansaldo defaults, the Jew requires a pound of the merchant's flesh, declining money tardily offered by Giannetto; but the usurer is outwitted by the lady of Belmonte, who has disguised herself as a lawyer for the purpose. She obtains from

Giannetto a ring which she had given him. After various recriminations, all is happily resolved: travelling to Belmonte, Ansaldo
(unlike Shakespeare's lonely Antonio) marries a servant-girl.

The casket story was ancient, but here Shakespeare's probable
source was another gathering of narratives, the mediæval *Gesta
romanorum*, as translated by Richard Robinson. Here a princess who
seeks to marry an emperor's son must choose between three
caskets, one of gold, one of silver, and one of lead. She correctly
chooses the lead casket and duly wins the prince. The Jessica-
Lorenzo sub-plot of *The Merchant of Venice* seems to derive from
Masuccio Salernitano's *Il novellino* (1476), in which a miser's
daughter elopes with a cavalier, stealing much of her father's
treasure. Anthony Munday's tale *Zelauto* (1580) had featured a trial
in which a miser is thwarted by two brides, who, disguised as
lawyers, save their husbands from mutilation by him. As in
Shakespeare, a salutary stipulation is that no drop of blood be shed.

Generally, when adapting and combining his source-materials,
Shakespeare provides unprecedented linguistic richness and the-
matic resonance, while characterisation becomes more vivid: his
Shylock is far more complex than is the usurer in *Il pecorone*.
Numerous details (such as the references to the Rialto, the *traghetto*,
the masques and the judicial system) lend credibility to the
Venetian setting. Even readers or playgoers who know well that
The Merchant of Venice is based on a wide range of legends, folk-tales
and romantic stories (not to mention centuries of prejudice) may
still assume that in certain obvious respects it tallies with historical
fact. The play was written around 1597, and we may assume that in
the real Venice of the late seventeenth century the Christians
undertook the merchant-venturing while the Jews, practising
usury, maintained a cultural separateness of a rather joyless and
puritanical kind. Brian Pullan's study, *Rich and Poor in Renaissance
Venice*, suggests that these assumptions are wrong.

Pullan shows that the Jews of Venice were subject to elaborate
and often punitive controls by the authorities. Those Jews were
obliged by law to maintain charitable and non-profitable banks to
provide loans to needy Christians at strictly-controlled low rates:
e.g. five per cent to cover expenses. In order to supply such banks,
Jews took to foreign trade. At a time (1590 to 1610) when many
Christian merchants, finding trade too risky, preferred to invest in

estates on the mainland, the Jews sent merchandise across the sea, particularly to the Turkish empire between Dalmatia and Constantinople. In some respects their risks were greater than Antonio's, for, in addition to the hazards of storm and tempest, their cargoes were subject to depredations by anti-Semitic Christian pirates, among them the Knights of St. John of Malta. During this period, the magistrates of Padua reported to the Venetian senate that Jewish merchants were markedly less rapacious than Christians:

> [T]he Jew is forbidden to invest his money in anything other than merchandise, and so long as he knows that trade is progressing and multiplying he is content with smaller gains than the Christian, who wishes to invest his money in estates, houses and other real property, and is not content with a little, but develops a voracious desire for gain.[5]

Venetian Jews were confined to a ghetto and subject to many humiliating restrictions. Numerous occupations were denied them, as they were prevented from infringing the Christian guilds' monopoly of manufacturing. For instance, they were forbidden to become tailors or to import new clothes.

> Behind these regulations, though it was never expressly acknowledged, there probably lay the desire to deny the Jews the satisfaction of creative work, and to thrust them into a position in which they appeared to be social parasites – dealers, middlemen and moneylenders, never producers. Anti-semitism itself foists upon the Jews the characteristics it later ascribes to their innate depravity. [6]

Nevertheless, occupations which remained open to them included those of physician, printer, bookseller, greengrocer – and musician. *The Merchant of Venice* memorably suggests that Christians (but not Jews) appreciate music, and are thus attuned to the celestial harmony which lies beyond this mortal vesture. Lorenzo explains the matter to Jessica:

> Here will we sit, and let the sounds of music
> Creep in our ears: soft stillness and the night
> Become the touches of sweet harmony . . . .
> There's not the smallest orb which thou behold'st

> But in his motion like an angel sings,
> Still quiring to the young-eyed cherubins.
> Such harmony is in immortal souls. . . .
> The man that hath no music in himself,
> Nor is not moved with concord of sweet sounds,
> Is fit for treasons, stratagems, and spoils; . . .
> Let no such man be trusted.

Such a treacherous man without music is clearly Shylock, who had commanded Jessica thus:

> Lock up my doors, and when you hear the drum
> And the vile squealing of the wry-necked fife,
> Clamber not you up to the casements then, . . .
> But stop my house's ears – I means my casements:
> Let not the sound of shallow fopp'ry enter
> My sober house.

In the historical Venice, however, the contrasting facts were these:

> [A]t the turn of the century, Jewish dancing masters, musicians and players were obviously sought-after by Christian pupils and audiences – as witness a licence prepared in September 1585 to authorize a Jew to enter the houses of eleven noblemen and five other persons 'to teach their children to sing, dance and play musical instruments, freely and without restraint'. Don Livio of Ferrara, a Jew resident in the Venetian Ghetto, received permission in the Carnival season to take his pupils or 'company' to dance in the houses of noblemen during the Carnivals of 1594 and 1595.[7]

Shylock has a Christian servant, Lancelet; but Patriarch Lorenzo Priuli had insisted in a memorandum of 1596–7 that Jews should not employ Christian servants or workmen, must not invite Christians to eat with them, and must wear yellow caps to mark them out as representatives of an accursed race. Yet these pariahs were nevertheless obliged to maintain charitable banks and to provide finance for the Venetian navy. Within their ghetto they still managed to organise fraternities for almsgiving, clothing the poor, lodging foreigners, and running a children's school and an academy.

In short, the myth propagated by Shakespeare (soon after the execution in London of Dr Roderigo López, a victim of anti-Semitic prejudice) offers some remarkable contrasts to the historical facts. Whether the effect of a particular production of *The Merchant of Venice* is anti-Semitic depends, obviously, on many factors, including the tenor of the performance, the predilections of members of the audience, and the historical and cultural context. Shakespeare's works owe their durability partly to the readiness of editors, actors, directors and commentators to interpret the plays so as to relate them to changing circumstances, and partly to the complexity of the plays themselves, which so frequently display qualities of ambiguity or paradox.

2

While much of *The Merchant of Venice* seems to draw on and augment an anti-Semitic tradition, numerous details seem repeatedly to hint at a contrasting drama, one more humane and progressive. There is a speech by Shylock which modulates into a defence of bloody revenge: 'If you poison us, do we not die? And if you wrong us, shall we not revenge?'; but, before that final modulation, it has made a resonant declaration of the human equality of Jew and Gentile:

> Hath not a Jew eyes? Hath not a Jew hands, organs, dimensions, senses, affections, passions? Fed with the same food, hurt with the same weapons, subject to the same diseases, healed by the same means, warmed and cooled by the same winter and summer, as a Christian is?

In the context of its times, this part of his speech makes a strikingly progressive utterance: it's one of those radiant moments when Shakespeare seems lucidly proleptic. Encompassed by Christians, Shylock can often seem the most credibly human of the characters. We know that he is constantly reviled. He says to Antonio:

> You call me disbeliever, cut-throat, dog,
> And spet upon my Jewish gaberdine,
> And all for use of that which is mine own.

Antonio's reply is uncompromising:

> I am as like to call thee so again,
> To spet on thee again, to spurn thee too . . . [8]

Again and again, Shylock is mocked and taunted, most harshly by
Gratiano at the trial. Like Lancelet, Gratiano suggests that the
only fit end for the Jewish 'dog' is the hangman's noose. The
sense of Shylock as lonely victim is acute when his daughter
Jessica elopes with a Christian: she has not only deserted her
father to marry a Gentile but has also, blithely, robbed him to go
on a spending-spree. Of course, Solanio and Salarino mock
Shylock's outburst of dismay, with its mixture of paternal and
financial lamentation; but some details give Shylock the full depth
of vulnerable humanity, most notably the detail of the turquoise.
Tubal says that one of Antonio's creditors displayed a ring 'that he
had of your daughter for a monkey'. Shylock replies:

> Out upon her! Thou torturest me, Tubal; it was my turquoise:
> I had it of Leah when I was a bachelor: I would not have given
> it for a wilderness of monkeys. [9]

The turquoise, we infer, was a love-token given him, when he
was a young man, by his fiancée; and it dawns on us that he is a
widower who has his sad memories – memories which, to his
daughter, mean nothing. Rings given by their wives to Bassanio
and Gratiano are surrendered by the two men to 'Balthazar' and
his clerk, occasioning embarrassment and recriminations; but the
love-tokens are eventually, amid laughter, restored. Shylock
never regains *his* ring. The eventual defeat of Shylock in court
can seem distastefully protracted and vindictive. Half his goods
are confiscated, to be held by Antonio 'in use'; then all his
possessions must be bequeathed to the spendthrift runaways,
Jessica and Lorenzo. The formerly melancholy and resigned
Antonio seems to undergo a remarkable recovery, characterized
by his detailed and decisive plans for disposing of Shylock's assets.
The decree that Shylock must 'presently become a Christian' is
another troubling feature. Editors claim that in Shakespeare's day
such a conversion would have been regarded (by Christians) as a
boon, saving the convert from the fires of hell and providing him
with the hope of heavenly salvation. But, given the detailed
evidence of Shylock's religious convictions, we sense that con-

version would be tantamount to a denaturing of him: we may regard him as, eventually, not a redeemed but a broken man. [10]

One large irony of the play is that Shylock has financed the endeavour that leads to his own downfall. His loan finances Bassanio's venture to Belmont, and Bassanio gains the long-sought 'golden fleece', Portia and her wealth. (He does so with the help of a bit of cheating on her part, for it is evident that the song 'Tell me where is Fancy bred' guides him to the correct casket. Music has its financial as well as its celestial associations.) In turn, Portia, loyal to her new husband and his dear friend, hastens to Venice to defeat the usurer. If, within the characterisation of the predominantly villainous Shylock, there are details which win an element of sympathy or understanding for him, so, within the characterisations of the predominantly decent Gentiles, we see details which may jar or repel us. Bassanio can seem insensitively eager to importune money from his lover, Antonio, and frank in his desire for a bride who is wealthy and not only virtuous. Lorenzo is untroubled by the fact that, when he elopes with Jessica, he is an accomplice in an act of theft. (She says, with remarkable frankness, 'I will . . . gild myself / With some moe ducats, and be with you straight': a ready suggestion of the power of gold coins to beautify her for her partner.) Portia, a stately and noble heroine, reveals a disturbing hypocrisy in racial matters. In Act 2, scene 1, she assures the Prince of Morocco that she is not racially prejudiced against him; but, behind his back, such prejudice emerges. She tells Nerissa:

> If he have the condition of a saint, and the complexion of a devil, I had rather he should shrive me than wive me.

And, after he is vanquished, she remarks: 'A gentle riddance . . . / Let all of his complexion choose me so.' (It's not an adequate defence to argue that such racial antipathy was then quite normal, for Desdemona easily transcends such prejudice in her love for Othello.) Then, at the trial scene, Bassanio says that if it would liberate Antonio, he would readily sacrifice to Shylock ('this devil') not only his own life but also that of Portia; and he is seconded by Gratiano, who similarly declares his readiness to sacrifice Nerissa for the same purpose. 'These be the Christian husbands!', remarks Shylock sardonically. He is granted a particu-

larly telling riposte when, declining to relinquish his claim to the
pound of flesh, he tells the court:

> You have among you many a purchased slave,
> Which, like your asses and your dogs and mules,
> You use in abject and in slavish parts,
> Because you bought them: shall I say to you,
> 'Let them be free, marry them to your heirs.
> Why sweat they under burdens? . . . ' You will answer,
> 'The slaves are ours.' So do I answer you.

Admittedly, Shylock had been no model employer to Lancelet
Gobbo; but Lancelet had contrived one of the most distasteful
'comic' scenes in Shakespeare when making cruel fun of his blind
and aged father by assuring the old man that his son was dead.

Thus, within the obvious drama in which Shylock is patently the
villain and his Gentile adversaries are evidently on the side of life,
love and generosity, there are hints – sometimes large hints – of an
alternative drama in which Shylock may be seen as a poignant and
even tragic victim, while his foes can be seen as his morally-suspect
vanquishers. If we look at the history of stage-productions of *The
Merchant of Venice*, we find that it was in the Romantic Age that
theatrical companies sought to develop these hints. It's understand-
able: one of the characteristics of Romantic culture is sympathy
with the underdog, with the isolated or estranged figure, and with
a person who, if partly villainous, is yet charismatic: we may think
of Ann Radcliffe's Montoni, of Emily Brontë's Heathcliff, and of
the claims by Blake and Shelley that Satan was the true hero of
Paradise Lost. Edmund Kean's enactment of Shylock, inaugurated
in January 1814, showed a man more sinned against than sinning:
passionate, intense, almost a martyr. G. H. Lewes claimed that the
English theatre had witnessed nothing more impressive than 'the
passionate recrimination and wild justice of argument in his "Hath
not a Jew eyes?" '; while William Hazlitt remarked: 'Certainly, our
sympathies are much oftener with him than with his enemies. He
is honest in his vices; they are hypocrites in their virtues.' [11]

Again, one of the most celebrated performances of the Victorian
era was Henry Irving's (November 1879 onwards), in which
Shylock was 'the type of a persecuted race; almost the only
gentleman in the play, and most ill-used'.[12] The text was ruthlessly

cut, but a new scene was added: a poignant one in which Shylock returns wearily home from a dinner and arrives at a deserted house, his daughter having fled. Furthermore, the effect of the trial scene was such that a critical commentator remarked:

[W]e momentarily expected the doge to rise exclaiming, 'My dear sir, pray accept the apology of the Court for any annoyance that this young person [Portia as Balthazar] has caused you. By all means take as much of Antonio as you think proper, and if we may throw in a prime cut off Bassanio and the whole of Gratiano we shall regard your acceptance of the same as a favour.'[13]

Later, at Stratford-upon-Avon in 1932, Theodore Komisarjevski directed a modernistic version which depicted Shylock as a man suffering injustice at the hands of a decadent bourgeoisie. Another notably sympathetic Shylock was that performed by Laurence Olivier in Jonathan Miller's National Theatre production of 1970: a bitter, neurotic figure, unhinged by his daughter's elopement. Again, cuts in the text came to Shylock's aid: the speech at 1.3.36–47 which includes 'I hate him for he is a Christian' was removed.

Alongside such versions which depicted Shylock relatively sympathetically, there have been numerous more conventional productions. While the latter may run the risk of appearing to propagate anti-Semitism, the former sometimes take liberties with the Shakespearian text in order to make it more congenial to predominant modern tastes. The 'merry bond' – the attempt to exact a pound of Christian flesh – cannot be 'adapted away'; nor can the insistent suggestion that Shylock, in his scheming cruelty, represents an epitome of Jewishness. Arnold Wesker's play, *The Merchant* (1977), attempted to redress the balance by taking salient elements of the plot of *The Merchant of Venice* and giving them a new interpretation.[14] The bond, the casket scene, the trial, the reversal achieved by Portia: they remain, but Wesker has transformed them. In his version, Shylock, though a moneylender, is a devoted bibliophile and lover of cultural history; Antonio is his dearest friend. Shylock, genial and warm-hearted, is eager to lend Antonio informally the requisite sum, but Antonio persuades him that the loan must be formalised legally, since a Venetian law insists that anyone who borrows from a Jew must enter a bond. So the stipulation of 'a pound of flesh' to be surrendered if the loan is not repaid is intended by Shylock and Antonio to mock a law which denies friendship between Jew and Gentile. In the event, when Antonio is unable to repay the loan, Shylock and Antonio agree to become martyrs. Antonio is prepared to die, and Shylock expects to be put to death for taking his friend's life. Both wish to abide by the laws of the Venetian state. Thanks to Portia's forensic skills, Antonio is saved; but the state confiscates all Shylock's goods, including his beloved library. To Antonio's grief, Shylock is now embittered and isolated.

The deep flaw in Wesker's play remains the 'merry bond', which the playwright boldly attempts to take over from Shakespeare and transform into true friendship's gesture of protest. As Wesker's Portia rightly says, 'A pound of flesh is a satanic price to conceive, even as a joke.' Since Antonio and Shylock are, in this version, such intelligent friends, the lethal riskiness of their chosen terms for the bond seems incredibly foolish. On the one hand, they feel that the laws are inhuman in their racism; on the other hand, they go to the court, ready to die, because the laws offer some protection to the Jews. The contradiction seems insuperable. Wesker has striven bravely, with much research and theatrical gusto, to transvalue Shakespeare's text, but the lethal bond is a knife directed at the heart of *The Merchant*'s dramatic plausibility.

3

Shakespeare's *The Merchant of Venice* has long been one of his more popular plays, frequently and successfully revived. One reason for the popularity is its rich variety. Realism, romance, lyricism, farce, folklore, bawdy comedy, forensic intensity, vividly diversified characterisation and firmly orchestrated themes: they are all there. Shylock dominates the play: this is the rôle for the aspiring actor. He is distinctive, vivid, larger than life, intense, didactically insistent, dogged, drily ironic, quietly venomous, passionately vengeful. The 1980 BBC production (made widely available as a video), with Warren Mitchell as Shylock, was exceptional in dramatising the full, uncut text. Mitchell, Jonathan Miller, the producer, and Jack Gold, the director, were all Jewish. This version made clear Shylock's mercurial variability and also the fact that he is a frustrated teacher: repeatedly, seeking to explain or justify his outlook, he tries to offer tuition (whether on thrift, domestic economy or retributive justice) to hearers who ignore, condemn or mock the tutor. He also tends to be in a minority of one, encompassed by those who, at best, barely tolerate him, and, at worst, gleefully bait and bully him. The play contains splendid speeches expressing romantic love and such civilised virtues as generosity, modesty and gratitude, so that the relatively harsh is repeatedly offset by the relatively benign. Though Shylock's vengeful malice is evident, he can be engaging because of it as well as in spite of it: we know him so fully that our knowledge veers towards complicity. His gamut of moods and tones make him one of the most interesting characters in Shakespeare for an audience to watch. When we respond to the play, our responses may be partly moral and political but also largely aesthetic; and by 'aesthetic' I mean that there is some suspension or subversion of moral judgements as matters of style, tone, eloquent expressiveness, emotional range and dramatic contrast come to the fore. Conspicuous artifice sustains the play's structure.[15] Just as the play offers intriguing combinations of the realistic and the implausible, of the mundane and the romantic, so it offers volatile mixtures of the ideologically problematic and the aesthetically escapist and entrancing. If some of its prejudices are daunting, it still sustains within itself bases for criticising those prejudices. If it bears clear signs of its date and ancestry, it also points forward to the future in ways which may both trouble and fascinate. Certainly our present era, in which intolerance, violence and decadence are matters of everyday report, can hardly claim superiority to Shakespeare's.

CEDRIC WATTS
University of Sussex

1 '[I]t's definitely an anti-semitic play, and I wouldn't do it', said the Jewish actor Maurice Schwartz (who had nevertheless played Shylock in Yiddish in 1921). See John Gross: *Shylock* (London: Chatto & Windus, 1992), p. 256.

2 See Chap. 18 of John Gross's *Shylock*. (The quotations are from pp. 288-90.)

3 Muriel Bradbrook: *Shakespeare and Elizabethan Poetry* [1951] (Harmondsworth: Penguin, 1964), p. 157.

4 *Shylock*, Chap. 18 (quotations from pp. 295 and 296).

5 Brian Pullan: *Rich and Poor in Renaissance Venice* (Oxford: Blackwell, 1971), p. 555.

6 *Rich and Poor in Renaissance Venice*, p. 552.

7 *Rich and Poor in Renaissance Venice*, p. 553.

8 I preserve 'spet', which is how the early texts spell 'spit'.

9 Muriel Bradbrook caustically remarks: 'Modern humanitarianism has run riot on Shylock . . . .Such an admission of conjugal fidelity is almost held to outweigh a taste for judicial murder' (*Shakespeare and Elizabethan Poetry*, p. 153).

10 James O'Connor's Shylock (New York, 1888) committed suicide in court, and Richard Mansfield's (New York, 1893) appeared to give himself a mortal wound with his knife before leaving the stage. (*Shylock*, pp. 150-51.)

11 Lewes: *On Actors and the Art of Acting* (London: Smith, Elder, 1875), p. 11. Hazlitt, review in *The Chronicle*, quoted in *The Merchant of Venice*, ed. John Russell Brown (London: Methuen, 1964), p. xxxiv.

12 Joseph Hatton: *Henry Irving's Impressions of America* (2 vols.; London: Sampson Low, Marston, Searle and Rivington, 1884), I, p. 265.

13 Graham Robertson: *Time Was* (London: Hamish Hamilton, 1931), p. 56.

14 The text was published in Wesker's *The Journalists / The Wedding Feast / The Merchant* (Harmondsworth: Penguin, 1980).

15 The patently lethal terms of the bond would surely have rendered it unlawful. Portia's quibble about 'no jot of blood' seems specious. If taking fractionally more or less than the pound of flesh rendered the taker liable to a death sentence, Shylock would surely have learnt this before the trial, and desisted. Similarly, if his seeking the life of a citizen rendered his life and goods forfeit, you would expect Shylock to have learnt this and desisted. The failure of Bassanio and Gratiano to recognise their own wives in court exemplifies the defeat of plausibility by stock convention. Antonio's ships are lost when the 'bond' plot requires it, but inexplicably reappear when the happy ending requires it.

FURTHER READING
(in chronological order)

Hermann Sinsheimer: *Shylock: The History of a Character; or, The Myth of the Jew*. London: Gollancz, 1947.

Narrative and Dramatic Sources of Shakespeare, Vol. I, ed. Geoffrey Bullough. London: Routledge & Kegan Paul; New York: Columbia University Press; 1957; rpt. 1964.

F. E. Halliday: *A Shakespeare Companion*. Harmondsworth: Penguin, 1964.

'Introduction' to *The Merchant of Venice*, ed. John Russell Brown. London: Methuen, 1964.

Brian Pullan: *Rich and Poor in Renaissance Venice*. Oxford: Blackwell, 1971.

Samuel Schoenbaum: *William Shakespeare: A Compact Documentary Life*. London and New York: Oxford University Press, 1977; rpt. 1987.

Norman Rabkin: 'Meaning and *The Merchant of Venice*' in *Shakespeare and the Problem of Meaning*. Chicago and London: University of Chicago Press, 1981.

The Cambridge Companion to Shakespeare Studies, ed. Stanley Wells. Cambridge: Cambridge University Press, 1986.

'Introduction' to William Shakespeare's *The Merchant of Venice*, ed. M. M. Mahood. Cambridge: Cambridge University Press, 1987.

Alan Sinfield: 'Making Space: Appropriation and Confrontation in Recent British Plays' in *The Shakespeare Myth*, ed. Graham Holderness. Manchester: Manchester University Press, 1988.

James C. Bulman: *The Merchant of Venice. Shakespeare in Performance*. Manchester and New York: Manchester University Press, 1991.

John Gross: *Shylock: Four Hundred Years in the Life of a Legend*. London: Chatto & Windus, 1992.

Russ McDonald: *The Bedford Companion to Shakespeare*. Basingstoke: Macmillan, 1996.

A Companion to Shakespeare, ed. David Scott Kastan. Malden, Mass., and Oxford: Blackwell, 1999.

NOTE ON SHAKESPEARE

Details of Shakespeare's early life are scanty. He was the son of a prosperous merchant of Stratford-upon-Avon, and tradition gives his date of birth as 23 April, 1564; certainly, three days later, he was christened at the parish church. It is likely that he attended the local Grammar School but had no university education. Of his early career there is no record, though John Aubrey states that he was a country schoolmaster. In 1582 Shakespeare married Anne Hathaway, with whom he had two daughters, Susanna and Judith, and a son, Hamnet, who died in 1596. How he became involved with the stage is uncertain, but he was sufficiently established as a playwright by 1592 to be criticised in print as a challengingly versatile 'upstart Crow'. He was a leading member of the Lord Chamberlain's company, which became the King's Men on the accession of James I in 1603. Being not only a playwright and actor but also a 'sharer' (one of the owners of the company, entitled to a share of the profits), Shakespeare prospered greatly, as is proven by the numerous records of his financial transactions. Towards the end of his life he loosened his ties with London and retired to New Place, his large property in Stratford which he had bought in 1597. He died on 23 April 1616, and is buried in the place of his baptism, Stratford's Holy Trinity Church. The earliest collected edition of his plays, the First Folio, was published in 1623, and its prefatory verse-tributes include Ben Jonson's famous declaration, 'He was not of an age, but for all time'.

ACKNOWLEDGEMENTS AND TEXTUAL NOTE

I have consulted numerous editions of *The Merchant of Venice*, notably those by Sir Arthur Quiller-Couch and John Dover Wilson (London: Cambridge University Press, 1926, rpt. 1962), John Russell Brown (the Arden Shakespeare: London: Methuen, 1964), M. M. Mahood (New Cambridge Shakespeare: Cambridge University Press, 1987), John F. Andrews (Everyman: London: Dent; Vermont: Tuttle; 1993), and Jay L. Halio (Oxford World's Classics: Oxford University Press, 1993). I am variously and particularly indebted to these editors: the Glossary, for example, adapts and revises Dover Wilson's.

When editing the play, I have taken careful account of the First Quarto and First Folio texts (1600 and 1623 respectively; commonly abbreviated as Q1 and F1). Almost all modern editors of *The Merchant of Venice* make a compromise between various elements, which include: (i) the material in the earliest printed versions, particularly in the highly-rated First Quarto text; (ii) what Shakespeare is thought to have intended (which sometimes differs from what those texts provide); and (iii) modern conventions of spelling, punctuation and presentation. My general rule has been to follow Q1 as closely as seems reasonable; but, obviously, what seems reasonable to one reader may not seem so to another. An illustration follows.

One famous editorial problem in *The Merchant of Venice* is that of the 'Three Sallies': Salarino, Salerio and Solanio. Some editors, following John Dover Wilson, reduce the three to two, believing that Shakespeare is unlikely to have invited confusion by using three similar names, and that the name 'Salarino' is merely a variant of 'Salerio'. Nevertheless, I follow M. M. Mahood and Jay L. Halio in retaining all three. My reasons include: the ambiguity of the evidence; my reluctance to depart from the nomenclature in the First Quarto and the First Folio; and the fact that Salerio is distinctively introduced in Act 3, scene 2, as '*a messenger from Venice*' (which would seem unnecessary if he were one of the Sallies we had met previously). For further discussion of this matter, see pp. 179–83 of Mahood's edition. I doubt that editors will find an elegant solution to the problem of the 'Three Sallies' – a problem which may well have been generated by a combination of the composer and the compositors, Shakespeare's celerity in composition creating ambiguities which were augmented in the printing-shop.

Another difficulty concerns the mobility of Salarino. In Act 2, scene 6, he apparently goes along to a masque with Jessica and Lorenzo; but in Act 2, scene 8, he reports the parting of Bassanio from Antonio, an event which, we may assume, either coincided with the masque or shortly preceded it. At 2.6.58–9, Lorenzo says: 'On, gentlemen, away; / Our masquing mates by this time for us stay.' Lorenzo then departs with Jessica and, it would seem, with the 'Sally' who is present – Salarino (if spelt a little erratically), according to Q1 and F1. Gratiano, starting to follow them, is suddenly detained by Antonio, who, arriving in haste, urges him to go to the ship which 'Bassanio presently will go aboard'. So how can Salarino report Bassanio's farewell? Mahood's solution is to postulate that, instead of accompanying Jessica and Lorenzo off-stage, Salarino remains alongside Gratiano as Antonio speaks. But what of those words 'On, gentlemen, away'? Mahood points out that although F1 has 'gentlemen', Q1 has the singular, 'gentleman'; and, thus, since Jessica is wearing masculine attire, 'gentleman' could be Lorenzo's jocular way of referring to her. This is ingenious; but, unfortunately, several objections come to mind. First, Jessica is disguised as a page-boy, not a gentleman. Secondly, 'gentlemen' seems an appropriate plural, since Lorenzo is aware of the presence of the two male friends who, dressed as masquers themselves, intend to accompany him to the masque. More objections arise when Antonio enters and detains Gratiano, saying 'Where are all the rest?'. This dialogue between these two men gives a strong impression that nobody else is present: for instance, Gratiano says: 'I am glad on't. I desire no more delight . . . '; not 'We are glad on't'; and, if Salarino were present, you would expect him to add his response to Gratiano's. A rescuer of consistency might suggest that when Antonio tells Gratiano, 'No masque tonight', he does not mean 'No masque for *you*, my friend, tonight, because the wind has changed, and you must sail with Bassanio'; he means 'No masque for *anyone* tonight, because – apart from the runaways – all the people who would have attended it (our friends and associates) are being re-directed to the harbour for the farewells there.' Thus, though Salarino has headed for the masque with Jessica and Lorenzo, he will soon find himself at the quayside. (As for Jessica and Lorenzo themselves: they elude pursuit by hastening – presumably overland – to Genoa, before coincidentally meeting Salerio and agreeing to proceed with him to Belmont.) If this reasoning fails to convince, one consolation is that though, as elsewhere in the play, an inconsistency may remain, such an inconsistency is peripheral to the main dramatic interest.

I hope that the present edition of *The Merchant of Venice* represents a reasonable and useful compromise between the old texts, Shakespeare's intentions (so far as they can be reasonably inferred) and modern requirements. The appended notes draw attention to some contentious readings. In any case, as you read the play, you will find that to some extent you are editing it to suit yourself, even as you are directing it in your imagination.

THE MERCHANT OF VENICE

CHARACTERS IN THE PLAY:

The Duke of Venice.

The Prince of Morocco ⎱ *suitors to Portia.*
The Prince of Arragon ⎰

ANTONIO, *a merchant of Venice.*

BASSANIO, *his friend, suitor to Portia.*

GRATIANO ⎱
SALARINO ⎰ *friends to Antonio and Bassanio.*
SOLANIO
SALERIO

LORENZO, *in love with Jessica.*

SHYLOCK, *a Jew.*

TUBAL, *another Jew, friend to Shylock.*

LANCELET GOBBO, *a clown, servant to Shylock.*

OLD GOBBO, *father to Lancelet.*

LEONARDO, *servant to Bassanio.*

BALTHAZAR ⎱ *servants to Portia.*
STEPHANO ⎰

PORTIA, *a lady of Belmont.*

NERISSA, *her waiting-maid.*

JESSICA, *daughter to Shylock.*

*Magnificoes of Venice, officers of the Court of Justice,
a jailor, servants, and other attendants.*

THE MERCHANT OF VENICE

ACT I, SCENE I.

A street in Venice.

Enter ANTONIO, SALARINO, *and* SOLANIO.

ANTONIO   In sooth, I know not why I am so sad.
It wearies me, you say it wearies you;
But how I caught it, found it, or came by it,
What stuff 'tis made of, whereof it is born,
I am to learn:
And such a want-wit sadness makes of me,
That I have much ado to know myself.

SALARINO   Your mind is tossing on the ocean,
There, where your argosies with portly sail[1] –
Like signiors and rich burghers on the flood,   10
Or as it were the pageants of the sea –
Do overpeer the petty traffickers
That curtsy to them, do them reverence,
As they fly by them with their woven wings.

SOLANIO   Believe me, sir, had I such venture forth,
The better part of my affections would
Be with my hopes abroad. I should be still
Plucking the grass to know where sits the wind,
Peering in maps for ports and piers and roads;
And every object that might make me fear   20
Misfortune to my ventures, out of doubt
Would make me sad.

SALARINO   My wind, cooling my broth,
Would blow me to an ague when I thought
What harm a wind too great might do at sea.
I should not see the sandy hour-glass run
But I should think of shallows and of flats,
And see my wealthy *Andrew* docked in sand,[2]
Vailing her high-top lower than her ribs
To kiss her burial.[3] Should I go to church
And see the holy edifice of stone,   30
And not bethink me straight of dangerous rocks,

          Which, touching but my gentle vessel's side,
          Would scatter all her spices on the stream,
          Enrobe the roaring waters with my silks,
          And, in a word, but even now worth this,
          And now worth nothing? Shall I have the thought
          To think on this, and shall I lack the thought
          That such a thing bechanced would make me sad?
          But tell not me; I know Antonio
          Is sad to think upon his merchandise.   40

ANTONIO   Believe me, no. I thank my fortune for it,
          My ventures are not in one bottom trusted,
          Nor to one place; nor is my whole estate
          Upon the fortune of this present year:
          Therefore my merchandise makes me not sad.

SOLANIO   Why then you are in love.

ANTONIO   Fie, fie.

SOLANIO   Not in love neither? Then let us say you are sad
          Because you are not merry; and 'twere as easy
          For you to laugh and leap, and say you are merry
          Because you are not sad. Now, by two-headed Janus, 50
          Nature hath framed strange fellows in her time:
          Some that will evermore peep through their eyes,
          And laugh like parrots at a bagpiper;
          And other of such vinegar aspect
          That they'll not show their teeth in way of smile,
          Though Nestor swear the jest be laughable.

          Enter BASSANIO, LORENZO, *and* GRATIANO.

          Here comes Bassanio, your most noble kinsman,
          Gratiano, and Lorenzo. Fare ye well,
          We leave you now with better company.

SALARINO I would have stayed till I had made you merry,   60
          If worthier friends had not prevented me.

ANTONIO   Your worth is very dear in my regard.
          I take it your own business calls on you,
          And you embrace th'occasion to depart.

SALARINO Good morrow, my good lords.

BASSANIO Good signiors both, when shall we laugh? Say, when?
          You grow exceeding strange: must it be so?

SALARINO	We'll make our leisures to attend on yours.
	[*Exeunt Salarino and Solanio.*]
LORENZO	My Lord Bassanio, since you have found Antonio,
	We two will leave you; but at dinner-time 70
	I pray you have in mind where we must meet.
BASSANIO	I will not fail you.
GRATIANO	You look not well, Signior Antonio;
	You have too much respect upon the world:
	They lose it that do buy it with much care.
	Believe me, you are marvellously changed.
ANTONIO	I hold the world but as the world, Gratiano:
	A stage, where every man must play a part,
	And mine a sad one.
GRATIANO	Let me play the fool,
	With mirth and laughter let old wrinkles come, 80
	And let my liver rather heat with wine
	Than my heart cool with mortifying groans.
	Why should a man whose blood is warm within
	Sit like his grandsire cut⁴ in alabaster,
	Sleep when he wakes, and creep into the jaundice
	By being peevish? I tell thee what, Antonio –
	I love thee, and it is my love that speaks –
	There are a sort of men whose visages
	Do cream and mantle like a standing pond,
	And do a wilful stillness entertain, 90
	With purpose to be dressed in an opinion
	Of wisdom, gravity, profound conceit,
	As who should say, 'I am Sir Oracle,
	And when I ope my lips, let no dog bark.'
	O, my Antonio, I do know of these
	That therefore only are reputed wise
	For saying nothing; when, I am very sure,
	If they should speak, would almost damn those ears
	Which, hearing them, would call their brothers fools.
	I'll tell thee more of this another time. 100
	But fish not with this melancholy bait
	For this fool gudgeon, this opinion.
	– Come, good Lorenzo. – Fare ye well awhile;
	I'll end my exhortation after dinner.

LORENZO   Well, we will leave you then till dinner-time.
           I must be one of these same dumb wise men,
           For Gratiano never lets me speak.

GRATIANO   Well, keep me company but two years moe,
           Thou shalt not know the sound of thine own tongue.

ANTONIO   Fare you well. I'll grow a talker for this gear.   110

GRATIANO   Thanks, i'faith, for silence is only commendable
           In a neat's tongue dried and a maid not vendible.[5]

                              [*Exeunt Gratiano and Lorenzo.*

ANTONIO   Is that anything now?

BASSANIO   Gratiano speaks an infinite deal of nothing, more than
           any man in all Venice. His reasons are as two grains of
           wheat hid in two bushels of chaff: you shall seek all day
           ere you find them, and when you have them they are
           not worth the search.

ANTONIO   Well, tell me now what lady is the same
           To whom you swore a secret pilgrimage,   120
           That you today promised to tell me of?

BASSANIO   'Tis not unknown to you, Antonio,
           How much I have disabled mine estate
           By something showing a more swelling port
           Than my faint means would grant continuance:
           Nor do I now make moan to be abridged
           From such a noble rate, but my chief care
           Is to come fairly off from the great debts
           Wherein my time, something too prodigal,
           Hath left me gaged. To you, Antonio,   130
           I owe the most in money and in love,
           And from your love I have a warranty
           To unburthen all my plots and purposes
           How to get clear of all the debts I owe.

ANTONIO   I pray you, good Bassanio, let me know it,
           And if it stand, as you yourself still do,
           Within the eye of honour, be assured,
           My purse, my person, my extremest means,
           Lie all unlocked to your occasions.

BASSANIO   In my school-days, when I had lost one shaft,   140
           I shot his fellow of the self-same flight
           The self-same way, with more advisèd watch,

THE MERCHANT OF VENICE

              To find the other forth; and by adventuring both,
              I oft found both. I urge this childhood proof,
              Because what follows is pure innocence.
              I owe you much, and, like a wilful youth,
              That which I owe is lost; but if you please
              To shoot another arrow that self way
              Which you did shoot the first, I do not doubt,
              As I will watch the aim, or to find both   150
              Or bring your latter hazard back again,
              And thankfully rest debtor for the first.

ANTONIO   You know me well, and herein spend but time
              To wind about my love with circumstance,
              And out of doubt you do me now more wrong
              In making question of my uttermost
              Than if you had made waste of all I have.
              Then do but say to me what I should do
              That in your knowledge may by me be done,
              And I am prest unto it: therefore, speak.   160

BASSANIO   In Belmont is a lady richly left,
              And she is fair, and, fairer than that word,
              Of wondrous virtues: sometimes from her eyes
              I did receive fair speechless messages.
              Her name is Portia, nothing undervalued
              To Cato's daughter, Brutus' Portia.[6]
              Nor is the wide world ignorant of her worth,
              For the four winds blow in from every coast
              Renownèd suitors, and her sunny locks
              Hang on her temples like a golden fleece,   170
              Which makes her seat of Belmont Colchos' strand,
              And many Jasons[7] come in quest of her.
              O my Antonio, had I but the means
              To hold a rival place with one of them,
              I have a mind presages me such thrift
              That I should questionless be fortunate.

ANTONIO   Thou know'st that all my fortunes are at sea,
              Neither have I money nor commodity
              To raise a present sum; therefore go forth,
              Try what my credit can in Venice do: 180
              That shall be racked, even to the uttermost,

To furnish thee to Belmont, to fair Portia.
Go, presently inquire, and so will I,
Where money is, and I no question make
To have it of my trust or for my sake.

                                                    [*Exeunt.*

SCENE 2.

Portia's house at Belmont.

Enter PORTIA *and* NERISSA.

PORTIA   By my troth, Nerissa, my little body is aweary of this
great world.

NERISSA   You would be, sweet madam, if your miseries were in
the same abundance as your good fortunes are: and yet,
for aught I see, they are as sick that surfeit with too
much as they that starve with nothing. It is no mean
happiness therefore to be seated in the mean:[8] super-
fluity comes sooner by white hairs, but competency
lives longer.

PORTIA   Good sentences, and well pronounced.   10

NERISSA   They would be better if well followed.

PORTIA   If to do were as easy as to know what were good to do,
chapels had been churches, and poor men's cottages
princes' palaces. It is a good divine that follows his own
instructions. I can easier teach twenty what were good
to be done, than be one of the twenty to follow mine
own teaching. The brain may devise laws for the blood,
but a hot temper leaps o'er a cold decree: such a hare is
madness the youth, to slip o'er the meshes of good
counsel the cripple. But this reasoning is not in the 20
fashion to choose me a husband. O me, the word
'choose'! I may neither choose whom I would, nor
refuse whom I dislike; so is the will of a living daughter
curbed by the will of a dead father. Is it not hard,
Nerissa, that I cannot choose one, nor refuse none?

NERISSA   Your father was ever virtuous, and holy men at their
death have good inspirations; therefore the lottery that

              he hath devised in these three chests of gold, silver and
              lead, whereof who chooses his meaning chooses you,
              will no doubt never be chosen by any rightly, but one 30
              whom you shall rightly love. But what warmth is there
              in your affection towards any of these princely suitors
              that are already come?

PORTIA   I pray thee over-name them, and as thou namest them,
              I will describe them, and according to my description
              level at my affection.

NERISSA   First there is the Neapolitan prince.

PORTIA   Ay, that's a colt indeed, for he doth nothing but talk of
              his horse, and he makes it a great appropriation to his
              own good parts that he can shoe him himself: I am much 40
              afeard my lady his mother played false with a smith.

NERISSA   Then is there the County Palatine.

PORTIA   He doth nothing but frown, as who should say, 'An
              you will not have me, choose!'[9] He hears merry tales,
              and smiles not. I fear he will prove the weeping
              philosopher[10] when he grows old, being so full of
              unmannerly sadness in his youth. I had rather be mar-
              ried to a death's-head with a bone in his mouth than to
              either of these: God defend me from these two!

NERISSA   How say you by the French lord, Monsieur Le Bon? 50

PORTIA   God made him, and therefore let him pass for a man. In
              truth, I know it is a sin to be a mocker, but he – why,
              he hath a horse better than the Neapolitan's, a better
              bad habit of frowning than the Count Palatine; he is
              every man in no man: if a throstle sing, he falls straight
              a-cap'ring: he will fence with his own shadow. If I
              should marry him, I should marry twenty husbands. If
              he would despise me, I would forgive him, for if he
              love me to madness, I shall never requite him.

NERISSA   What say you then to Falconbridge, the young baron 60
              of England?

PORTIA   You know I say nothing to him, for he understands
              not me, nor I him: he hath neither Latin, French, nor
              Italian, and you will come into the court and swear
              that I have a poor pennyworth in the English. He is a
              proper man's picture, but, alas, who can converse with

a dumb-show? How oddly he is suited! I think he bought his doublet in Italy, his round hose in France, his bonnet in Germany, and his behaviour everywhere.   70

NERISSA   What think you of the Scottish lord, his neighbour?

PORTIA   That he hath a neighbourly charity[11] in him, for he borrowed a box of the ear of the Englishman, and swore he would pay him again when he was able: I think the Frenchman became his surety, and sealed under for another.[12]

NERISSA   How like you the young German, the Duke of Saxony's nephew?

PORTIA   Very vilely in the morning when he is sober, and most vilely in the afternoon when he is drunk: when he is   80 best, he is a little worse than a man, and when he is worst, he is little better than a beast. An the worst fall that ever fell, I hope I shall make shift to go without him.

NERISSA   If he should offer to choose, and choose the right casket, you should refuse to perform your father's will, if you should refuse to accept him.

PORTIA   Therefore, for fear of the worst, I pray thee set a deep glass of Rhenish wine on the contrary casket, for if the devil be within, and that temptation without, I know   90 he will choose it. I will do anything, Nerissa, ere I will be married to a sponge.

NERISSA   You need not fear, lady, the having any of these lords: they have acquainted me with their determinations, which is indeed to return to their home, and to trouble you with no more suit, unless you may be won by some other sort than your father's imposition depending on the caskets.

PORTIA   If I live to be as old as Sibylla,[13] I will die as chaste as Diana,[14] unless I be obtained by the manner of my   100 father's will. I am glad this parcel of wooers are so reasonable, for there is not one among them but I dote on his very absence; and I pray God grant them a fair departure.

NERISSA   Do you not remember, lady, in your father's time, a

Venetian, a scholar and a soldier, that came hither in
company of the Marquis of Montferrat?

PORTIA   Yes, yes, it was Bassanio, as I think so was he called.

NERISSA   True, madam, he, of all the men that ever my foolish
eyes looked upon, was the best deserving a fair lady.   110

PORTIA   I remember him well, and I remember him worthy of
thy praise.

A servant enters.

How now! what news?

SERVANT   The four strangers seek for you, madam, to take their
leave; and there is a forerunner come from a fifth, the
Prince of Morocco, who brings word the Prince his
master will be here tonight.

PORTIA   If I could bid the fifth welcome with so good heart as I
can bid the other four farewell, I should be glad of his
approach. If he have the condition of a saint, and the   120
complexion of a devil,[15] I had rather he should shrive
me than wive me.
Come, Nerissa. Sirrah, go before:
Whiles we shut the gate upon one wooer,
Another knocks at the door.

                       [*Exeunt.*

SCENE 3.

A street in Venice.

Enter BASSANIO *and* SHYLOCK.

SHYLOCK   Three thousand ducats[16] – well.

BASSANIO   Ay, sir, for three months.

SHYLOCK   For three months – well.

BASSANIO   For the which, as I told you, Antonio shall be bound.

SHYLOCK   Antonio shall become bound – well.

BASSANIO   May you stead me? Will you pleasure me? Shall I know
your answer?

SHYLOCK   Three thousand ducats for three months, and Antonio
bound.

BASSANIO   Your answer to that.   10

SHYLOCK	Antonio is à good man.
BASSANIO	Have you heard any imputation to the contrary?
SHYLOCK	Ho no, no, no, no: my meaning in saying he is a good man, is to have you understand me that he is suffi-cient. Yet his means are in supposition: he hath an argosy bound to Tripolis, another to the Indies; I understand moreover upon the Rialto, he hath a third at Mexico, a fourth for England, and other ventures he hath squandered abroad. But ships are but boards, sailors but men; there be land-rats and water-rats, 20 land-thieves and water-thieves – I mean pirates – and then there is the peril of waters, winds, and rocks. The man is, notwithstanding, sufficient. Three thousand ducats; I think I may take his bond.
BASSANIO	Be assured you may.
SHYLOCK	I will be assured I may: and, that I may be assured, I will bethink me. May I speak with Antonio?
BASSANIO	If it please you to dine with us.
SHYLOCK	Yes, to smell pork, to eat of the habitation which your prophet the Nazarite conjured the devil into.[17] I will 30 buy with you, sell with you, talk with you, walk with you, and so following: but I will not eat with you, drink with you, nor pray with you.[18] What news on the Rialto? Who is he comes here?

Enter ANTONIO.

BASSANIO	This is Signior Antonio. [*He talks with Antonio.*
SHYLOCK	[*aside:*] How like a fawning publican[19] he looks!

I hate him for he is a Christian;
But more, for that in low simplicity
He lends out money gratis, and brings down
The rate of usance here with us in Venice.   40
If I can catch him once upon the hip,
I will feed fat the ancient grudge I bear him.
He hates our sacred nation, and he rails,
Even there where merchants most do congregate,
On me, my bargains, and my well-won thrift,
Which he calls interest. Cursed be my tribe
If I forgive him!

BASSANIO	Shylock, do you hear?

SHYLOCK   I am debating of my present store,
And by the near guess of my memory
I cannot instantly raise up the gross   50
Of full three thousand ducats: what of that?
Tubal,[20] a wealthy Hebrew of my tribe,
Will furnish me; but soft, how many months
Do you desire?
[*To Antonio:*]   Rest you fair, good signior,
Your worship was the last man in our mouths.

ANTONIO   Shylock, albeit I neither lend nor borrow
By taking nor by giving of excess,
Yet to supply the ripe wants of my friend
I'll break a custom.
[*To Bassanio:*]   Is he yet possessed
How much ye would?

SHYLOCK   Ay, ay, three thousand ducats. 60

ANTONIO   And for three months.

SHYLOCK   I had forgot; three months; you told me so.
Well then, your bond; and let me see – but hear you,
Methought you said you neither lend nor borrow
Upon advantage.

ANTONIO   I do never use it.

SHYLOCK   When Jacob grazed his uncle Laban's sheep,
This Jacob from our holy Abram was
(As his wise mother wrought in his behalf)
The third possessor; ay, he was the third[21] –

ANTONIO   And what of him? did he take interest?   70

SHYLOCK   No, not take interest – not as you would say
Directly interest; mark what Jacob did.
When Laban and himself were compromised
That all the eanlings which were streaked and pied
Should fall as Jacob's hire, the ewes, being rank
In end of autumn, turnèd to the rams,
And when the work of generation was
Between these woolly breeders in the act,
The skilful shepherd pilled me certain wands,
And, in the doing of the deed of kind,   80
He stuck them up before the fulsome ewes,
Who, then conceiving, did in eaning time

	Fall parti-coloured lambs, and those were Jacob's.[22]
	This was a way to thrive, and he was blest;
	And thrift is blessing if men steal it not.
ANTONIO	This was a venture, sir, that Jacob served for:
	A thing not in his power to bring to pass,
	But swayed and fashioned by the hand of heaven.
	Was this inserted to make interest good?
	Or is your gold and silver ewes and rams?
SHYLOCK	I cannot tell; I make it breed as fast;
	But note me, signior.
ANTONIO	Mark you this, Bassanio,
	The devil can cite Scripture for his purpose.[23]
	An evil soul, producing holy witness,
	Is like a villain with a smiling cheek,
	A goodly apple rotten at the heart.
	O, what a goodly outside falsehood hath!
SHYLOCK	Three thousand ducats: 'tis a good round sum.
	Three months from twelve, then, let me see, the rate —
ANTONIO	Well, Shylock, shall we be beholding to you?
SHYLOCK	Signior Antonio, many a time and oft
	In the Rialto you have rated me
	About my moneys and my usances:
	Still have I borne it with a patient shrug,
	For suff'rance is the badge of all our tribe.
	You call me misbeliever, cut-throat, dog,
	And spet upon my Jewish gaberdine,
	And all for use of that which is mine own.
	Well then, it now appears you need my help:
	Go to then, you come to me, and you say,
	'Shylock, we would have moneys' — you say so!
	You that did void your rheum upon my beard,
	And foot me as you spurn a stranger cur
	Over your threshold — moneys is your suit.
	What should I say to you? Should I not say,
	'Hath a dog money? Is it possible
	A cur can lend three thousand ducats?' Or
	Shall I bend low, and in a bondman's key,
	With bated breath, and whisp'ring humbleness,
	Say this:

90

100

110

120

            'Fair sir, you spet on me on Wednesday last;
            You spurned me such a day; another time
            You called me dog: and for these courtesies
            I'll lend you thus much moneys'?

ANTONIO   I am as like to call thee so again,
            To spet on thee again, to spurn thee too.
            If thou wilt lend this money, lend it not
            As to thy friends – for when did friendship take
            A breed for barren metal[24] of his friend? –
            But lend it rather to thine enemy,   130
            Who if he break, thou mayst with better face
            Exact the penalty.

SHYLOCK   Why, look you, how you storm!
            I would be friends with you, and have your love,
            Forget the shames that you have stained me with,
            Supply your present wants, and take no doit
            Of usance for my moneys, and you'll not hear me:
            This is kind I offer.

ANTONIO   This were kindness.

SHYLOCK   This kindness will I show.
            Go with me to a notary, seal me there
            Your single bond,[25] and, in a merry sport,   140
            If you repay me not on such a day,
            In such a place, such sum or sums as are
            Expressed in the condition, let the forfeit
            Be nominated for an equal pound
            Of your fair flesh, to be cut off and taken
            In what part of your body pleaseth me.

ANTONIO   Content, in faith; I'll seal to such a bond,
            And say there is much kindness in the Jew.

BASSANIO   You shall not seal to such a bond for me;
            I'll rather dwell in my necessity.   150

ANTONIO   Why, fear not, man, I will not forfeit it.
            Within these two months, that's a month before
            This bond expires, I do expect return
            Of thrice three times the value of this bond.

SHYLOCK   O father Abram, what these Christians are,
            Whose own hard dealing teaches them suspect
            The thoughts of others! Pray you, tell me this:

If he should break his day, what should I gain
By the exaction of the forfeiture?
A pound of man's flesh, taken from a man,   160
Is not so estimable, profitable neither,
As flesh of muttons, beefs, or goats. I say
To buy his favour, I extend this friendship.
If he will take it, so; if not, adieu;
And, for my love, I pray you wrong me not.

ANTONIO   Yes, Shylock, I will seal unto this bond.

SHYLOCK   Then meet me forthwith at the notary's,
Give him direction for this merry bond,
And I will go and purse the ducats straight,
See to my house (left in the fearful guard   170
Of an unthrifty knave); and presently
I will be with you.

ANTONIO   Hie thee, gentle Jew.

                                            [*Exit Shylock.*
The Hebrew will turn Christian – he grows kind.

BASSANIO   I like not fair terms and a villain's mind.

ANTONIO   Come on; in this there can be no dismay:
My ships come home a month before the day.

                                            [*Exeunt.*

ACT 2, SCENE I.

Portia's house at Belmont.

Enter the Prince of Morocco, a tawny Moor all in white,
and three or four followers accordingly, with PORTIA,
NERISSA, *and their train.*

MOROCCO   Mislike me not for my complexion,
The shadowed livery of the burnished sun,[26]
To whom I am a neighbour and near bred.
Bring me the fairest creature northward born,
Where Phoebus' fire scarce thaws the icicles,
And let us make incision for your love,
To prove whose blood is reddest, his or mine.
I tell thee, lady, this aspect of mine
Hath feared the valiant;[27] by my love, I swear
The best-regarded virgins of our clime   10
Have loved it too: I would not change this hue,
Except to steal your thoughts, my gentle queen.

PORTIA   In terms of choice I am not solely led
By nice direction of a maiden's eyes;
Besides, the lott'ry of my destiny
Bars me the right of voluntary choosing;
But if my father had not scanted me
And hedged me by his wit to yield myself
His wife who wins me by that means I told you,
Yourself, renownèd prince, then stood as fair   20
As any comer I have looked on yet
For my affection.

MOROCCO   Even for that I thank you.
Therefore, I pray you, lead me to the caskets
To try my fortune. By this scimitar,
That slew the Sophy and a Persian prince
That won three fields of Sultan Solyman,[28]
I would o'erstare the sternest eyes that look,
Outbrave the heart most daring on the earth,
Pluck the young sucking cubs from the she-bear,

Yea, mock the lion when a roars for prey,   30
To win the lady. But, alas the while!
If Hercules and Lichas[29] play at dice
Which is the better man, the greater throw
May turn by fortune from the weaker hand:
So is Alcides beaten by his page,[30]
And so may I, blind Fortune leading me,
Miss that which one unworthier may attain,
And die with grieving.

PORTIA   You must take your chance,
And either not attempt to choose at all,
Or swear, before you choose, if you choose wrong,   40
Never to speak to lady afterward
In way of marriage. Therefore be advised.

MOROCCO   Nor will not. Come, bring me unto my chance.

PORTIA   First, forward to the temple. After dinner
Your hazard shall be made.

MOROCCO   Good fortune then,
To make me blest or cursèd'st among men!

                                                              [Exeunt.

SCENE 2.

A street in Venice.

Enter LANCELET GOBBO.[31]

LANCELET   Certainly my conscience will serve me to run from this
Jew my master. The fiend is at mine elbow, and tempts
me, saying to me, 'Gobbo, Lancelet Gobbo, good
Lancelet', or 'good Gobbo', or 'good Lancelet Gobbo,
use your legs, take the start; run away'. My conscience
says, 'No; take heed, honest Lancelet, take heed, honest
Gobbo', or as aforesaid, 'honest Lancelet Gobbo, do
not run, scorn running with thy heels'. Well, the most
courageous fiend bids me pack. 'Fia!' says the fiend;
'away!' says the fiend, 'for the heavens, rouse up a brave   10
mind', says the fiend, 'and run'. Well, my conscience,
hanging about the neck of my heart, says very wisely to
me: 'My honest friend, Lancelet, being an honest

man's son' – or rather an honest woman's son, for
indeed my father did something smack, something
grow to; he had a kind of taste; well, my conscience
says, 'Lancelet, budge not.' 'Budge', says the fiend.
'Budge not', says my conscience. 'Conscience', say I,
'you counsel well.' 'Fiend', say I, 'you counsel well.'
To be ruled by my conscience, I should stay with the 20
Jew my master, who – God bless the mark! – is a kind
of devil; and to run away from the Jew, I should be
ruled by the fiend, who, saving your reverence, is the
devil himself. Certainly, the Jew is the very devil
incarnation;[32] and, in my conscience, my conscience is
but a kind of hard conscience, to offer to counsel me
to stay with the Jew. The fiend gives the more
friendly counsel. I will run, fiend; my heels are at your
commandment; I will run.

Enter OLD GOBBO *with a basket.*

OLD GOBBO Master young-man, you, I pray you, which is the way 30
to Master Jew's?

LANCELET [*aside:*] O heavens, this is my true-begotten father, who
being more than sand-blind, high gravel-blind,[33]
knows me not. I will try confusions with him.

OLD GOBBO Master, young gentleman, I pray you which is the way
to Master Jew's?

LANCELET Turn up on your right hand at the next turning, but at
the next turning of all on your left; marry, at the very
next turning turn of no hand, but turn down indirectly
to the Jew's house. 40

OLD GOBBO Be God's sonties, 'twill be a hard way to hit. Can you
tell me whether one Lancelet that dwells with him,
dwell with him or no?

LANCELET Talk you of young Master Lancelet? [*Aside:*] Mark me
now, now will I raise the waters. – Talk you of young
Master Lancelet?

OLD GOBBO No 'master', sir, but a poor man's son. His father,
though I say't, is an honest exceeding poor man, and,
God be thanked, well to live.

LANCELET Well, let his father be what a will, we talk of young 50
Master Lancelet.

OLD GOBBO Your worship's friend and Lancelet, sir.

LANCELET But I pray you, ergo old man, ergo I beseech you, talk
you of young Master Lancelet.

OLD GOBBO Of Lancelet, an't please your mastership.

LANCELET Ergo, Master Lancelet. Talk not of Master Lancelet,
father, for the young gentleman – according to fates
and destinies, and such odd sayings, the Sisters Three,[34]
and such branches of learning – is indeed deceased, or
as you would say in plain terms, gone to heaven.   60

OLD GOBBO Marry, God forbid! The boy was the very staff of my
age, my very prop.

LANCELET [aside:] Do I look like a cudgel or a hovel-post, a staff or
a prop? – Do you know me, father?

OLD GOBBO Alack the day, I know you not, young gentleman, but
I pray you tell me, is my boy – God rest his soul! – alive
or dead?

LANCELET Do you not know me, father?

OLD GOBBO Alack, sir, I am sand-blind: I know you not.

LANCELET Nay, indeed, if you had your eyes, you might fail of 70
the knowing me: it is a wise father that knows his own
child.[35] Well, old man, I will tell you news of your son.
[He kneels.] Give me your blessing. Truth will come to
light, murder cannot be hid long; a man's son may, but
in the end truth will out.

OLD GOBBO Pray you, sir, stand up. I am sure you are not Lancelet,
my boy.

LANCELET Pray you, let's have no more fooling about it, but give
me your blessing: I am Lancelet, your boy that was,
your son that is, your child that shall be.   80

OLD GOBBO I cannot think you are my son.

LANCELET I know not what I shall think of that: but I am Lancelet
the Jew's man, and I am sure Margery, your wife, is my
mother.

OLD GOBBO Her name is Margery, indeed. I'll be sworn, if thou be
Lancelet, thou art mine own flesh and blood. [He feels
back of Lancelet's head.] Lord worshipped might he be!
What a beard hast thou got! Thou hast got more hair
on thy chin than Dobbin my fill-horse has on his tail.[36]

LANCELET It should seem then that Dobbin's tail grows backward. 90

I am sure he had more hair of his tail than I have of my
face, when I last saw him.

OLD GOBBO   Lord, how art thou changed! How dost thou and thy
master agree? I have brought him a present. How 'gree
you now?

LANCELET   Well, well. But, for mine own part, as I have set up my
rest[37] to run away, so I will not rest till I have run some
ground. My master's a very Jew. Give him a present?
Give him a halter! I am famished in his service. You
may tell every finger I have with my ribs. Father, I am   100
glad you are come. Give me your present to one
Master Bassanio, who indeed gives rare new liveries. If
I serve not him, I will run as far as God has any ground.
O rare fortune! Here comes the man: to him, father,
for I am a Jew if I serve the Jew any longer.

Enter BASSANIO *with* LEONARDO *and a follower or two.*

BASSANIO   [*talking to a servant:*] You may do so, but let it be so
hasted that supper be ready at the farthest by five of the
clock. See these letters delivered, put the liveries to
making, and desire Gratiano to come anon to my
lodging.   [*Exit servant.* 110

LANCELET   To him, father.

OLD GOBBO   God bless your worship!

BASSANIO   Gramercy, wouldst thou aught with me?

OLD GOBBO   Here's my son, sir, a poor boy –

LANCELET   Not a poor boy, sir, but the rich Jew's man that would,
sir, as my father shall specify –

OLD GOBBO   He hath a great infection,[38] sir, as one would say, to
serve –

LANCELET   Indeed, the short and the long is, I serve the Jew, and
have a desire as my father shall specify –   110

OLD GOBBO   His master and he, saving your worship's reverence,
are scarce cater-cousins –

LANCELET   To be brief, the very truth is, that the Jew having done
me wrong, doth cause me, as my father being I hope
an old man shall frutify[39] unto you –

OLD GOBBO   I have here a dish of doves that I would bestow upon
your worship, and my suit is –

LANCELET   In very brief, the suit is impertinent[40] to myself, as your
            worship shall know by this honest old man, and though
            I say it, though old man, yet (poor man) my father.   130

BASSANIO   One speak for both. What would you?

LANCELET   Serve you, sir.

OLD GOBBO   That is the very defect[41] of the matter, sir.

BASSANIO   I know thee well; thou hast obtained thy suit.
            Shylock, thy master, spoke with me this day,
            And hath preferred thee, if it be preferment
            To leave a rich Jew's service to become
            The follower of so poor a gentleman.

LANCELET   The old proverb[42] is very well parted between my
            master Shylock and you, sir: you have 'the grace of   140
            God', sir, and he hath 'enough'.

BASSANIO   Thou speak'st it well; go, father, with thy son.
            Take leave of thy old master, and inquire
            My lodging out. [To a follower:] Give him a livery
            More guarded[43] than his fellows': see it done.

LANCELET   Father, in. I cannot get a service, no, I have ne'er a
            tongue in my head! [He looks at his palm:] Well, if any
            man in Italy have a fairer table[44] which doth offer to
            swear upon a book, I shall have good fortune. Go to,
            here's a simple line of life,[45] here's a small trifle of wives   150
            – alas, fifteen wives is nothing: eleven widows, and
            nine maids, is a simple coming-in for one man; and then
            to scape drowning thrice, and to be in peril of my life
            with the edge of a feather-bed: here are simple scapes.
            Well, if Fortune be a woman, she's a good wench for
            this gear. Father, come. I'll take my leave of the Jew in
            the twinkling.[46]   [Exeunt Lancelet and Old Gobbo.

BASSANIO   I pray thee, good Leonardo, think on this.
            These things being bought and orderly bestowed,
            Return in haste, for I do feast tonight   160
            My best-esteemed acquaintance; hie thee, go.

LEONARDO   My best endeavours shall be done herein.

                        Enter GRATIANO

GRATIANO   Where's your master?

LEONARDO   Yonder, sir, he walks. [Exit Leonardo.

GRATIANO	Signior Bassanio!
BASSANIO	Gratiano!
GRATIANO	I have a suit to you.
BASSANIO	You have obtained it.
GRATIANO	You must not deny me – I must go with you to Belmont.
BASSANIO	Why, then you must. But hear thee, Gratiano,

Thou art too wild, too rude, and bold of voice:
Parts that become thee happily enough,   170
And in such eyes as ours appear not faults;
But where thou art not known, why, there they show
Something too liberal. Pray thee, take pain
To allay with some cold drops of modesty
Thy skipping spirit, lest through thy wild behaviour
I be misconstered in the place I go to,
And lose my hopes.

GRATIANO   Signior Bassanio, hear me.
If I do not put on a sober habit,
Talk with respect, and swear but now and then,
Wear prayer-books in my pocket, look demurely –   180
Nay more, while grace is saying, hood mine eyes
Thus with my hat, and sigh, and say 'amen',
Use all the observance of civility,
Like one well studied in a sad ostent
To please his grandam – never trust me more.

BASSANIO Well, we shall see your bearing.

GRATIANO Nay, but I bar tonight: you shall not gauge me
By what we do tonight.

BASSANIO   No, that were pity,
I would entreat you rather to put on
Your boldest suit of mirth, for we have friends   190
That purpose merriment. But fare you well;
I have some business.

GRATIANO And I must to Lorenzo and the rest;
But we will visit you at supper-time.

                                                [Exeunt.

SCENE 3.

Shylock's house.

Enter JESSICA *and* LANCELET.

JESSICA I am sorry thou wilt leave my father so:
Our house is hell, and thou, a merry devil,
Didst rob it of some taste of tediousness.
But fare thee well; there is a ducat for thee.
And, Lancelet, soon at supper shalt thou see
Lorenzo, who is thy new master's guest.
Give him this letter, do it secretly,
And so farewell: I would not have my father
See me talk with thee.

LANCELET Adieu; tears exhibit[47] my tongue. Most beautiful pa- 10
gan, most sweet Jew, if a Christian do not play the
knave and get thee, I am much deceived. But adieu;
these foolish drops do something drown my manly
spirit; adieu!   [*Exit.*

JESSICA Farewell, good Lancelet.
Alack, what heinous sin is it in me
To be ashamed to be my father's child!
But though I am a daughter to his blood,
I am not to his manners. O Lorenzo,
If thou keep promise, I shall end this strife,   20
Become a Christian and thy loving wife.
                                                  [*Exit.*

SCENE 4.

A street in Venice.

Enter GRATIANO, LORENZO, SALARINO *and* SOLANIO.

LORENZO   Nay, we will slink away in supper-time,
           Disguise us at my lodging, and return
           All in an hour.
GRATIANO   We have not made good preparation.
SALARINO   We have not spoke as yet of torch-bearers.
SOLANIO   'Tis vile, unless it may be quaintly ordered,
           And better in my mind not undertook.
LORENZO   'Tis now but four o'clock: we have two hours
           To furnish us.

Enter LANCELET

                    Friend Lancelet, what's the news?
LANCELET   [*giving him a letter:*] An it shall please you to break up   10
           this, it shall seem to signify.
LORENZO   I know the hand: in faith, 'tis a fair hand,
           And whiter than the paper it writ on
           Is the fair hand that writ.
GRATIANO   Love-news, in faith.
LANCELET   By your leave, sir.
LORENZO   Whither goest thou?
LANCELET   Marry, sir, to bid my old master the Jew to sup tonight
           with my new master the Christian.
LORENZO   Hold here, take this. [*He gives him money.*]
                         Tell gentle Jessica
           I will not fail her; speak it privately; Go. [*Lancelet goes.*   20
           Gentlemen,
           Will you prepare you for this masque tonight?
           I am provided of a torch-bearer.
SALARINO   Ay, marry, I'll be gone about it straight.
SOLANIO   And so will I.
LORENZO   Meet me and Gratiano
           At Gratiano's lodging some hour hence.
SALARINO   'Tis good we do so.   [*Exeunt Salarino and Solanio.*

GRATIANO	Was not that letter from fair Jessica?
LORENZO	I must needs tell thee all. She hath directed
	How I shall take her from her father's house, 30
	What gold and jewels she is furnished with,
	What page's suit she hath in readiness.
	If e'er the Jew her father come to heaven,
	It will be for his gentle daughter's sake;
	And never dare misfortune cross her foot
	Unless she do it under this excuse,
	That she is issue to a faithless Jew.
	Come, go with me; peruse this as thou goest.
	Fair Jessica shall be my torch-bearer. 40

[*Exeunt.*

SCENE 5.

The street before Shylock's house.

Enter SHYLOCK *and* LANCELET.

SHYLOCK	Well, thou shalt see – thy eyes shall be thy judge –
	The difference of old Shylock and Bassanio.
	– What, Jessica! – Thou shalt not gormandize,
	As thou hast done with me – What, Jessica! –
	And sleep and snore, and rend apparel out.
	– Why, Jessica, I say!
LANCELET	Why, Jessica!
SHYLOCK	Who bids thee call? I do not bid thee call.
LANCELET	Your worship was wont to tell me I could do nothing
	without bidding.

Enter JESSICA.

JESSICA	Call you? What is your will?	10
SHYLOCK	I am bid forth to supper, Jessica.	
	There are my keys. But wherefore should I go?	
	I am not bid for love; they flatter me.	
	But yet I'll go in hate, to feed upon	
	The prodigal Christian. Jessica, my girl,	
	Look to my house. I am right loath to go;	
	There is some ill a-brewing towards my rest,	
	For I did dream of money-bags tonight.	

LANCELET	I beseech you, sir, go: my young master doth expect
	your reproach.[48]
SHYLOCK	So do I his.
LANCELET	And they have conspired together. I will not say you
	shall see a masque, but if you do, then it was not for
	nothing that my nose fell a-bleeding on Black Monday
	last, at six o'clock i'th' morning, falling out that year on
	Ash Wednesday was four year, in th'afternoon.[49]
SHYLOCK	What, are there masques? Hear you me, Jessica:
	Lock up my doors, and when you hear the drum
	And the vile squealing of the wry-necked fife,[50]
	Clamber not you up to the casements then,
	Nor thrust your head into the public street
	To gaze on Christian fools with varnished faces:
	But stop my house's ears – I mean my casements:
	Let not the sound of shallow fopp'ry enter
	My sober house. By Jacob's staff [51] I swear
	I have no mind of feasting forth tonight;
	But I will go. Go you before me, sirrah:
	Say I will come.
LANCELET	I will go before, sir. [*Aside to Jessica:*] Mistress, look out
	at window, for all this –
	There will come a Christian by,
	Will be worth a Jewess' eye.[52] [*Exit.*
SHYLOCK	What says that fool of Hagar's offspring,[53] ha?
JESSICA	His words were, 'Farewell, mistress'; nothing else.
SHYLOCK	The patch is kind enough, but a huge feeder,
	Snail-slow in profit, and he sleeps by day
	More than the wild-cat: drones hive not with me:
	Therefore I part with him, and part with him
	To one that I would have him help to waste
	His borrowed purse. Well, Jessica, go in.
	Perhaps I will return immediately.
	Do as I bid you, shut doors after you:
	'Fast bind, fast find',[54]
	A proverb never stale in thrifty mind. [*Exit.*
JESSICA	Farewell; and if my fortune be not crost,
	I have a father, you a daughter, lost.
	[*Exit.*

Line numbers: 20, 30, 40, 50

SCENE 6.

Enter, as masquers, GRATIANO *and* SALARINO.[55]

GRATIANO This is the pent-house under which Lorenzo
          Desired us to make stand.
SALARINO   His hour is almost past.
GRATIANO And it is marvel he out-dwells his hour,
          For lovers ever run before the clock.
SALARINO O, ten times faster Venus' pigeons[56] fly
          To seal love's bonds new-made, than they are wont
          To keep obligèd faith unforfeited![57]
GRATIANO That ever holds: who riseth from a feast
          With that keen appetite that he sits down?
          Where is the horse that doth untread again   10
          His tedious measures with the unbated fire
          That he did pace them first? All things that are,
          Are with more spirit chasèd than enjoyed.
          How like a younger[58] or a prodigal
          The scarfèd bark puts from her native bay,
          Hugged and embracèd by the strumpet wind!
          How like the prodigal doth she return,[59]
          With over-weathered ribs and raggèd sails,
          Lean, rent and beggared by the strumpet wind!

Enter LORENZO.

SALARINO Here comes Lorenzo; more of this hereafter.   20
LORENZO   Sweet friends, your patience for my long abode.
          Not I, but my affairs, have made you wait:
          When you shall please to play the thieves for wives,
          I'll watch as long for you then. Approach;
          Here dwells my father Jew. Ho! Who's within?

Enter JESSICA *above, clad as a boy.*

JESSICA   Who are you? Tell me, for more certainty,
          Albeit I'll swear that I do know your tongue.
LORENZO   Lorenzo, and thy love.
JESSICA   Lorenzo, certain, and my love indeed,
          For who love I so much? And now who knows   30

But you, Lorenzo, whether I am yours?

LORENZO Heaven and thy thoughts are witness that thou art.

JESSICA Here, catch this casket, it is worth the pains.

                          [*Lorenzo catches it.*

I am glad 'tis night, you do not look on me,
For I am much ashamed of my exchange;
But love is blind, and lovers cannot see
The pretty follies that themselves commit;
For if they could, Cupid himself would blush
To see me thus transformèd to a boy.

LORENZO Descend, for you must be my torch-bearer.   40

JESSICA What, must I hold a candle to my shames?
They in themselves, good sooth, are too too light.[60]
Why, 'tis an office of discovery, love,
And I should be obscured.[61]

LORENZO   So are you, sweet,
Even in the lowly garnish[62] of a boy.
But come at once,
For the close night doth play the runaway,[63]
And we are stayed for at Bassanio's feast.

JESSICA I will make fast the doors, and gild myself
With some moe ducats, and be with you straight.   50

                               [*Exit above.*

GRATIANO Now, by my hood, a gentile and no Jew.

LORENZO Beshrew me but I love her heartily,
For she is wise, if I can judge of her,
And fair she is, if that mine eyes be true,
And true she is, as she hath proved herself:
And therefore, like herself, wise, fair, and true,
Shall she be placèd in my constant soul.

               Enter JESSICA *below.*

What, art thou come? On, gentlemen, away;
Our masquing mates by this time for us stay.

                     [*Exit with Jessica and Salarino.*

                   Enter ANTONIO.

ANTONIO Who's there?   60

GRATIANO Signior Antonio?

ANTONIO Fie, fie, Gratiano! Where are all the rest?

'Tis nine o'clock: our friends all stay for you.
No masque tonight: the wind is come about;
Bassanio presently will go aboard.
I have sent twenty out to seek for you.

GRATIANO I am glad on't. I desire no more delight
Than to be under sail and gone tonight.

[*Exeunt.*

SCENE 7.

Portia's house at Belmont.

Enter PORTIA *with the Prince of Morocco and both their trains.*

PORTIA Go, draw aside the curtains, and discover
The several caskets to this noble prince.
Now make your choice.

MOROCCO The first, of gold, who this inscription bears,
'Who chooseth me shall gain what many men desire.'
The second, silver, which this promise carries,
'Who chooseth me shall get as much as he deserves.'
This third, dull lead, with warning all as blunt,
'Who chooseth me must give and hazard all he hath.'
How shall I know if I do choose the right?   10

PORTIA The one of them contains my picture, Prince.
If you choose that, then I am yours withal.

MOROCCO Some god direct my judgement! Let me see;
I will survey th'inscriptions back again.
What says this leaden casket?
'Who chooseth me must give and hazard all he hath.'
Must give – for what? For lead? Hazard for lead?
This casket threatens. Men that hazard all
Do it in hope of fair advantages:
A golden mind stoops not to shows of dross.   20
I'll then nor give nor hazard aught for lead.
What says the silver with her virgin hue?⁶⁴
'Who chooseth me shall get as much as he deserves.'
As much as he deserves! Pause there, Morocco,
And weigh thy value with an even hand.
If thou beest rated by thy estimation,

Thou dost deserve enough; and yet enough
May not extend so far as to the lady:
And yet to be afeard of my deserving
Were but a weak disabling of myself.   30
As much as I deserve! Why, that's the lady.
I do in birth deserve her, and in fortunes,
In graces, and in qualities of breeding;
But more than these, in love I do deserve.
What if I strayed no further, but chose here?
Let's see once more this saying graved in gold:
'Who chooseth me shall gain what many men desire.'
Why, that's the lady; all the world desires her.
From the four corners of the earth they come
To kiss this shrine, this mortal breathing saint.   40
The Hyrcanian deserts and the vasty wilds
Of wide Arabia are as throughfares now
For princes to come view fair Portia.
The watery kingdom, whose ambitious head
Spets in the face of heaven, is no bar
To stop the foreign spirits, but they come,
As o'er a brook, to see fair Portia.
One of these three contains her heavenly picture.
Is't like that lead contains her? 'Twere damnation
To think so base a thought; it were too gross   50
To rib her cerecloth in the óbscure grave.[65]
Or shall I think in silver she's immured,
Being ten times undervalued to tried gold?
O sinful thought! Never so rich a gem
Was set in worse than gold. They have in England
A coin that bears the figure of an angel[66]
Stampèd in gold, but that's insculped upon;
But here an angel in a golden bed
Lies all within. Deliver me the key:
Here do I choose, and thrive I as I may!   60

PORTIA   There, take it, Prince, and if my form lie there,
          Then I am yours.   [*He unlocks the golden casket.*
MOROCCO   O hell! What have we here?
          A carrion Death, within whose empty eye
          There is a written scroll. I'll read the writing.

'All that glisters is not gold,
Often have you heard that told.
Many a man his life hath sold,
But my outside to behold.
Gilded tombs do worms infold.
Had you been as wise as bold,   70
Young in limbs, in judgement old,
Your answer had not been inscrolled.
Fare you well, your suit is cold.'
Cold, indeed, and labour lost.
Then, farewell heat, and welcome frost.
Portia, adieu. I have too grieved a heart
To take a tedious leave: thus losers part.   [*Exit.*

PORTIA A gentle riddance. Draw the curtains, go.
Let all of his complexion choose me so.

                                                   [*Exeunt.*

SCENE 8.

A street in Venice.

Enter SALARINO *and* SOLANIO.

SALARINO Why, man, I saw Bassanio under sail;
With him is Gratiano gone along;
And in their ship I am sure Lorenzo is not.

SOLANIO The villain Jew with outcries raised the Duke,
Who went with him to search Bassanio's ship.

SALARINO He came too late: the ship was under sail;
But there the Duke was given to understand
That in a gondylo were seen together
Lorenzo and his amorous Jessica.
Besides, Antonio certified the Duke   10
They were not with Bassanio in his ship.

SOLANIO I never heard a passion so confused,
So strange, outrageous, and so variable,
As the dog Jew did utter in the streets:
'My daughter! O my ducats! O my daughter!
Fled with a Christian! O my Christian ducats!

Justice! The law! My ducats, and my daughter!
A sealèd bag, two sealèd[67] bags of ducats,
Of double ducats, stol'n from me by my daughter!
And jewels – two stones, two rich and precious stones, 20
Stol'n by my daughter! Justice! Find the girl!
She hath the stones upon her, and the ducats!'

SALARINO   Why, all the boys in Venice follow him,
Crying, 'His stones, his daughter, and his ducats!'

SOLANIO   Let good Antonio look he keep his day,
Or he shall pay for this.

SALARINO   Marry, well remembered:
I reasoned with a Frenchman yesterday,
Who told me, in the narrow seas that part
The French and English, there miscarrièd
A vessel of our country richly fraught: 30
I thought upon Antonio when he told me,
And wished in silence that it were not his.

SOLANIO   You were best to tell Antonio what you hear;
Yet do not suddenly, for it may grieve him.

SALARINO   A kinder gentleman treads not the earth.
I saw Bassanio and Antonio part:
Bassanio told him he would make some speed
Of his return; he answered, ' Do not so.
Slubber not business for my sake, Bassanio,
But stay the very riping of the time.   40
And for the Jew's bond which he hath of me,
Let it not enter in your mind of love:
Be merry, and employ your chiefest thoughts
To courtship, and such fair ostents of love
As shall conveniently become you there.'
And even there, his eye being big with tears,
Turning his face, he put his hand behind him,
And with affection wondrous sensible
He wrung Bassanio's hand, and so they parted.

SOLANIO   I think he only loves the world for him.   50
I pray thee, let us go and find him out,
And quicken his embracèd heaviness
With some delight or other.

SALARINO   Do we so.   [Exeunt.

SCENE 9.

Portia's house at Belmont.

Enter NERISSA *and a Servitor.*

NERISSA   Quick, quick, I pray thee, draw the curtain straight.
           The Prince of Arragon hath ta'en his oath,
           And comes to his election presently.

Enter the Prince of Arragon, his train, and PORTIA.

PORTIA   Behold, there stand the caskets, noble Prince.
           If you choose that wherein I am contained,
           Straight shall our nuptial rites be solemnized;
           But, if you fail, without more speech, my lord,
           You must be gone from hence immediately.

ARRAGON   I am enjoined by oath to observe three things:
           First, never to unfold to anyone   10
           Which casket 'twas I chose; next, if I fail
           Of the right casket, never in my life
           To woo a maid in way of marriage;
           Lastly,
           If I do fail in fortune of my choice,
           Immediately to leave you and be gone.

PORTIA   To these injunctions everyone doth swear
           That comes to hazard for my worthless self.

ARRAGON   And so have I addressed me. Fortune now
           To my heart's hope! Gold, silver, and base lead.   20
           'Who chooseth me must give and hazard all he hath.'
           You shall look fairer, ere I give or hazard.
           What says the golden chest? Ha! Let me see:
           'Who chooseth me shall gain what many men desire.'
           What many men desire! That 'many' may be meant
           By the fool multitude, that choose by show,
           Not learning more than the fond eye doth teach,
           Which pries not to th'interior, but like the martlet
           Builds in the weather on the outward wall,
           Even in the force and road of casualty.   30
           I will not choose what many men desire,

Because I will not jump with common spirits,
And rank me with the barbarous multitudes.
Why, then to thee, thou silver treasure-house!
Tell me once more what title thou dost bear:
'Who chooseth me shall get as much as he deserves.'
And well said too; for who shall go about
To cozen Fortune and be honourable
Without the stamp of merit? Let none presume
To wear an undeservèd dignity.   40
O, that estates, degrees and offices
Were not derived corruptly, and that clear honour
Were purchased by the merit of the wearer.
How many then should cover that stand bare!
How many be commanded that command!
How much low peasantry would then be gleaned
From the true seed of honour! And how much honour
Picked from the chaff and ruin of the times,
To be new varnished! Well, but to my choice.
'Who chooseth me shall get as much as he deserves.'   50
I will assume desert. Give me a key for this,
And instantly unlock my fortunes here.
                                    [*He opens the silver casket.*

PORTIA   Too long a pause for that which you find there.
ARRAGON   What's here? The portrait of a blinking idiot,
            Presenting me a schedule! I will read it.
            How much unlike art thou to Portia!
            How much unlike my hopes and my deservings!
            'Who chooseth me shall have as much as he deserves.'
            Did I deserve no more than a fool's head?
            Is that my prize? Are my deserts no better?   60
PORTIA   To offend and judge are distinct offices,[68]
            And of opposèd natures.
ARRAGON   What is here?
            'The fire[69] seven times tried this;
            Seven times tried that judgement is,
            That did never choose amiss.[70]
            Some there be that shadows kiss,
            Such have but a shadow's bliss.
            There be fools alive, iwis,

Silvered o'er, and so was this.
Take what wife you will to bed,   70
I will ever be your head.
So be gone; you are sped.'

Still more fool I shall appear
By the time I linger here.
With one fool's head I came to woo,
But I go away with two.
Sweet, adieu! I'll keep my oath,
Patiently to bear my wroth.[71]

[Exeunt Arragon and his train.

PORTIA   Thus hath the candle singed the moth.
O, these deliberate fools! When they do choose,   80
They have the wisdom by their wit to lose.[72]

NERISSA   The ancient saying is no heresy:
Hanging and wiving goes by destiny.

PORTIA   Come, draw the curtain, Nerissa.

Enter messenger.

MESSENGER Where is my lady?

PORTIA   Here: what would my lord?

MESSENGER Madam, there is alighted at your gate
A young Venetian, one that comes before
To signify th'approaching of his lord,
From whom he bringeth sensible regreets:
To wit (besides commends and courteous breath),   90
Gifts of rich value. Yet I have not seen
So likely an ambassador of love.
A day in April never came so sweet,
To show how costly summer was at hand,
As this fore-spurrer comes before his lord.

PORTIA   No more, I pray thee. I am half afeard
Thou wilt say anon he is some kin to thee,
Thou spend'st such high-day wit in praising him.
Come, come, Nerissa, for I long to see
Quick Cupid's post that comes so mannerly.   100

NERISSA   Bassanio, Lord Love, if thy will it be!

[Exeunt.

ACT 3, SCENE 1.

A street in Venice.

Enter SOLANIO *and* SALARINO.

SOLANIO   Now, what news on the Rialto?

SALARINO   Why, yet it lives there unchecked that Antonio hath a ship of rich lading wracked on the narrow seas: the Goodwins, I think they call the place: a very dangerous flat, and fatal, where the carcases of many a tall ship lie buried, as they say, if my gossip Report be an honest woman of her word.

SOLANIO   I would she were as lying a gossip in that, as ever knapped ginger, or made her neighbours believe she wept for the death of a third husband. But it is true,   10 without any slips of prolixity or crossing the plain highway of talk, that the good Antonio, the honest Antonio – O, that I had a title good enough to keep his name company –

SALARINO   Come, the full stop.

SOLANIO   Ha! what sayest thou? Why, the end is, he hath lost a ship.

SALARINO   I would it might prove the end of his losses.

SOLANIO   Let me say 'amen' betimes, lest the devil cross my prayer, for here he comes in the likeness of a Jew.   20

Enter SHYLOCK.

How now, Shylock! What news among the merchants?

SHYLOCK   You knew, none so well, none so well as you, of my daughter's flight.

SALARINO   That's certain. I, for my part, knew the tailor that made the wings she flew withal.

SOLANIO   And Shylock, for his own part, knew the bird was fledge, and then it is the complexion of them all to leave the dam.

SHYLOCK   She is damned for it.

SALARINO   That's certain, if the devil may be her judge.   30

SHYLOCK   My own flesh and blood to rebel!

SOLANIO   Out upon it, old carrion, rebels it at these years?[73]

SHYLOCK   I say, my daughter is my flesh and blood.

SALARINO   There is more difference between thy flesh and hers
             than between jet and ivory; more between your bloods
             than there is between red wine and Rhenish. But tell
             us, do you hear whether Antonio have had any loss at
             sea or no?

SHYLOCK   There I have another bad match: a bankrout, a
             prodigal, who dare scarce show his head on the Rialto, a   40
             beggar that was used to come so smug upon the Mart.
             Let him look to his bond. He was wont to call me usurer:
             let him look to his bond. He was wont to lend money for
             a Christian courtesy: let him look to his bond.

SALARINO   Why, I am sure, if he forfeit, thou wilt not take his
             flesh: what's that good for?

SHYLOCK   To bait fish withal. If it will feed nothing else, it will
             feed my revenge. He hath disgraced me, and hindered
             me half a million, laughed at my losses, mocked at my
             gains, scorned my nation, thwarted my bargains,   50
             cooled my friends, heated mine enemies – and what's
             his reason? I am a Jew. Hath not a Jew eyes? Hath not
             a Jew hands, organs, dimensions, senses, affections,
             passions? Fed with the same food, hurt with the same
             weapons, subject to the same diseases, healed by the
             same means, warmed and cooled by the same winter
             and summer, as a Christian is? If you prick us, do we
             not bleed? If you tickle us, do we not laugh? If you
             poison us, do we not die? And if you wrong us, shall
             we not revenge? If we are like you in the rest, we will   60
             resemble you in that. If a Jew wrong a Christian, what
             is his humility? Revenge. If a Christian wrong a Jew,
             what should his sufferance be by Christian example?
             Why, revenge. The villainy you teach me I will ex-
             ecute, and it shall go hard but I will better the
             instruction.

                         Enter a servant.

SERVANT   Gentlemen, my master Antonio is at his house, and
             desires to speak with you both.

SALARINO   We have been up and down to seek him.

Enter TUBAL.

SOLANIO   Here comes another of the tribe; a third cannot be 70
              matched, unless the devil himself turn Jew.
                     [*Exeunt Solanio, Salarino and the servant.*

SHYLOCK   How now, Tubal! What news from Genoa? Hast thou
              found my daughter?

TUBAL   I often came where I did hear of her, but cannot find
              her.

SHYLOCK   Why there, there, there, there! A diamond gone, cost
              me two thousand ducats in Frankfort. The curse never
              fell upon our nation till now;[74] I never felt it till now.
              Two thousand ducats in that, and other precious,
              precious jewels. I would my daughter were dead at my 80
              foot, and the jewels in her ear! Would she were
              hearsed at my foot, and the ducats in her coffin! No
              news of them? Why so? And I know not what's spent
              in the search: why, thou loss upon loss! The thief gone
              with so much, and so much to find the thief, and no
              satisfaction, no revenge, nor no ill luck stirring but
              what lights o' my shoulders, no sighs but o' my breath-
              ing, no tears but o' my shedding.

TUBAL   Yes, other men have ill luck too. Antonio, as I heard in
              Genoa, –   90

SHYLOCK   What, what, what? Ill luck, ill luck?

TUBAL   – hath an argosy cast away, coming from Tripolis.

SHYLOCK   I thank God, I thank God! Is it true? Is it true?

TUBAL   I spoke with some of the sailors that escaped the wrack.

SHYLOCK   I thank thee, good Tubal. Good news, good news –
              ha, ha! – here in Genoa.[75]

TUBAL   Your daughter spent in Genoa, as I heard, one night,
              fourscore ducats.

SHYLOCK   Thou stick'st a dagger in me. I shall never see my gold
              again. Fourscore ducats at a sitting: fourscore ducats! 100

TUBAL   There came divers of Antonio's creditors in my company
              to Venice, that swear he cannot choose but break.

SHYLOCK   I am very glad of it. I'll plague him, I'll torture him. I
              am glad of it.

TUBAL   One of them showed me a ring that he had of your
              daughter for a monkey.

SHYLOCK   Out upon her! Thou torturest me, Tubal; it was my
          turquoise:[76] I had it of Leah when I was a bachelor: I
          would not have given it for a wilderness of monkeys.

TUBAL   But Antonio is certainly undone.   110

SHYLOCK   Nay, that's true, that's very true. Go Tubal, fee me an
          officer, bespeak him a fortnight before. I will have the
          heart of him if he forfeit, for were he out of Venice I
          can make what merchandise I will. Go, Tubal, and
          meet me at our synagogue. Go, good Tubal; at our
          synagogue, Tubal.

                                               [Exeunt.

                        SCENE 2.

                  Portia's house at Belmont.

          Enter BASSANIO, PORTIA, GRATIANO, NERISSA
                      and attendants.

PORTIA   [to Bassanio:] I pray you, tarry: pause a day or two
          Before you hazard, for in choosing wrong
          I lose your company; therefore, forbear awhile.
          There's something tells me (but it is not love)[77]
          I would not lose you, and you know yourself
          Hate counsels not in such a quality;
          But lest you should not understand me well –
          And yet a maiden hath no tongue but thought[78] –
          I would detain you here some month or two
          Before you venture for me. I could teach you   10
          How to choose right, but then I am forsworn;
          So will I never be; so may you miss me,
          But if you do, you'll make me wish a sin,
          That I had been forsworn. Beshrew your eyes,
          They have o'er-looked me and divided me.
          One half of me is yours, the other half yours –
          Mine own, I would say; but if mine, then yours,
          And so all yours. O, these naughty times
          Put bars between the owners and their rights,
          And so though yours, not yours. Prove it so,[79]   20

Let Fortune go to hell for it, not I.
I speak too long, but 'tis to peize[80] the time,
To eke it and to draw it out in length,
To stay you from election.

BASSANIO   Let me choose:
For as I am, I live upon the rack.[81]

PORTIA   Upon the rack, Bassanio? Then confess
What treason there is mingled with your love.

BASSANIO   None but that ugly treason of mistrust,
Which makes me fear th'enjoying of my love.[82]
There may as well be amity and life   30
'Tween snow and fire as treason and my love.

PORTIA   Ay, but I fear you speak upon the rack,
Where men enforcèd do speak any thing.

BASSANIO   Promise me life, and I'll confess the truth.

PORTIA   Well then, confess and live.

BASSANIO   'Confess' and 'love'
Had been the very sum of my confession:
O happy torment, when my torturer
Doth teach me answers for deliverance!
But let me to my fortune and the caskets.

PORTIA   Away then! I am locked in one of them.   40
If you do love me, you will find me out.
Nerissa and the rest, stand all aloof.
Let music sound while he doth make his choice:
Then if he lose, he makes a swan-like end,[83]
Fading in music. That the comparison
May stand more proper, my eye shall be the stream
And wat'ry death-bed for him. He may win,
And what is music then? Then music is
Even as the flourish when true subjects bow
To a new-crownèd monarch: such it is,   50
As are those dulcet sounds in break of day
That creep into the dreaming bridegroom's ear,
And summon him to marriage. Now he goes,
With no less presence, but with much more love,
Than young Alcides, when he did redeem
The virgin tribute paid by howling Troy
To the sea-monster. I stand for sacrifice;

The rest aloof are the Dardanian wives,
With bleared visages, come forth to view
The issue of th'exploit.[84] Go, Hercules: 60
Live thou, I live. With much much more dismay
I view the fight than thou that mak'st the fray.

Music and a song, before[85] BASSANIO *comments on the caskets to himself.*

SINGER   Tell me where is Fancy[86] bred,
                    Or in the heart, or in the head?
                    How begot, how nourishèd?[87]
OTHER SINGERS   Reply, reply.
SINGER   It is engendered in the eyes,
                    With gazing fed; and Fancy dies
                    In the cradle where it lies.
                          Let us all ring Fancy's knell: 70
                          I'll begin it: Ding, dong, bell.
OTHER SINGERS   Ding, dong, bell.

BASSANIO   So may the outward shows be least themselves:
                  The world is still deceived with ornament.
                  In law, what plea so tainted and corrupt,
                  But, being seasoned with a gracious voice,
                  Obscures the show of evil? In religion,
                  What damnèd error, but some sober brow
                  Will bless it, and approve it with a text,
                  Hiding the grossness with fair ornament?   80
                  There is no vice so simple, but assumes
                  Some mark of virtue on his outward parts.
                  How many cowards, whose hearts are all as false
                  As stairs of sand, wear yet upon their chins
                  The beards of Hercules and frowning Mars,
                  Who, inward searched, have livers white as milk?
                  And these assume but valour's excrement
                  To render them redoubted.[88] Look on beauty,
                  And you shall see 'tis purchased by the weight,[89]
                  Which therein works a miracle in nature,   90
                  Making them lightest[90] that wear most of it:
                  So are those crispèd snaky golden locks
                  Which make such wanton gambols with the wind,

Upon supposèd fairness, often known
To be the dowry of a second head,
The skull that bred them in the sepulchre.
Thus ornament is but the guiled shore
To a most dangerous sea; the beauteous scarf
Veiling an Indian beauty; in a word,
The seeming truth which cunning times put on   100
To entrap the wisest. Then,[91] thou gaudy gold,
Hard food for Midas,[92] I will none of thee;
Nor none of thee, thou pale and common drudge
'Tween man and man; but thou, thou meagre lead,
Which rather threaten'st than dost promise aught,
Thy plainness moves me more than eloquence,
And here choose I – joy be the consequence!

PORTIA   How all the other passions fleet to air,
As doubtful thoughts, and rash-embraced despair,
And shudd'ring fear and green-eyed jealousy!   110
O love, be moderate, allay thy ecstasy,
In measure rain thy joy, scant this excess!
I feel too much thy blessing: make it less,
For fear I surfeit!

BASSANIO   [opening the leaden casket:] What find I here?
Fair Portia's counterfeit. What demi-god
Hath come so near creation? Move these eyes?
Or whether, riding on the balls of mine,
Seem they in motion? Here are severed lips,
Parted with sugar breath: so sweet a bar
Should sunder such sweet friends. Here in her hairs   120
The painter plays the spider, and hath woven
A golden mesh t'entrap the hearts of men
Faster than gnats in cobwebs. But her eyes!
How could he see to do them? Having made one,
Methinks it should have power to steal both his,
And leave itself unfurnished. Yet look, how far
The substance of my praise doth wrong this shadow
In underprizing it, so far this shadow
Doth limp behind the substance. Here's the scroll,
The continent and summary of my fortune.   130

'You that choose not by the view,
Chance as fair and choose as true:[93]
Since this fortune falls to you,
Be content, and seek no new.
If you be well pleased with this,
And hold your fortune for your bliss,
Turn you where your lady is,
And claim her with a loving kiss.'
A gentle scroll. Fair lady, by your leave,
I come by note, to give and to receive.   140
Like one of two contending in a prize,
That thinks he hath done well in people's eyes,
Hearing applause and universal shout,
Giddy in spirit, still gazing in a doubt
Whether those peals of praise be his or no,
So, thrice-fair lady, stand I, even so,
As doubtful whether what I see be true,
Until confirmed, signed, ratified by you.

PORTIA   You see me, Lord Bassanio, where I stand,
Such as I am. Though for myself alone   150
I would not be ambitious in my wish
To wish myself much better, yet for you
I would be trebled twenty times myself —
A thousand times more fair, ten thousand times
More rich —
That, only to stand high in your account,
I might in virtues, beauties, livings, friends,
Exceed account; but the full sum of me
Is sum of something,[94] which, to term in gross,
Is an unlessoned girl, unschooled, unpractised;   160
Happy in this, she is not yet so old
But she may learn; happier than this,
She is not bred so dull but she can learn;
Happiest of all is that her gentle spirit
Commits itself to yours to be directed,
As from her lord, her governor, her king.
Myself and what is mine, to you and yours
Is now converted. But now I was the lord
Of this fair mansion, master of my servants,

	Queen o'er myself; and even now, but now,	170
	This house, these servants, and this same myself,	
	Are yours, my lord's! I give them with this ring,	
	Which when you part from, lose, or give away,	
	Let it presage the ruin of your love,	
	And be my vantage to exclaim on you.	
BASSANIO	Madam, you have bereft me of all words.	
	Only my blood speaks to you in my veins,	
	And there is such confusion in my powers,	
	As after some oration fairly spoke	
	By a belovèd prince there doth appear	180
	Among the buzzing pleasèd multitude,	
	Where every something, being blent together,	
	Turns to a wild of nothing, save of joy	
	Expressed and not expressed. But when this ring	
	Parts from this finger, then parts life from hence.	
	O, then be bold to say Bassanio's dead.	
NERISSA	My lord and lady, it is now our time,	
	That have stood by and seen our wishes prosper,	
	To cry 'Good joy, good joy, my lord and lady!'	
GRATIANO	My Lord Bassanio, and my gentle lady,	190
	I wish you all the joy that you can wish,	
	For I am sure you can wish none from me;[95]	
	And, when your honours mean to solemnise	
	The bargain of your faith, I do beseech you,	
	Even at that time I may be married too.	
BASSANIO	With all my heart, so thou canst get a wife.	
GRATIANO	I thank your lordship, you have got me one.	
	My eyes, my lord, can look as swift as yours:	
	You saw the mistress, I beheld the maid;	
	You loved, I loved; for intermission	200
	No more pertains to me, my lord, than you.	
	Your fortune stood upon the caskets there,	
	And so did mine too, as the matter falls:	
	For wooing here until I sweat again,	
	And swearing till my very roof was dry	
	With oaths of love, at last – if promise last –	
	I got a promise of this fair one here,	
	To have her love, provided that your fortune	

Achieved her mistress.

PORTIA   Is this true, Nerissa?

NERISSA   Madam, it is, so you stand pleased withal.   210

BASSANIO   And do you, Gratiano, mean good faith?

GRATIANO   Yes, faith, my lord.

BASSANIO   Our feast shall be much honoured in your marriage.

GRATIANO   [to Nerissa:] We'll play with them, the first boy for a
thousand ducats.

NERISSA   What! and stake down?

GRATIANO   No, we shall ne'er win at that sport, and stake down.[96]

Enter LORENZO, JESSICA, *and* SALERIO, *a messenger from Venice.*

But who comes here? Lorenzo and his infidel?
What, and my old Venetian friend, Salerio?

BASSANIO   Lorenzo and Salerio, welcome hither,   220
If that the youth of my new interest here
Have power to bid you welcome. [*To Portia:*]
                              By your leave,
I bid my very friends and countrymen,
Sweet Portia, welcome.

PORTIA   So do I, my lord.
They are entirely welcome.

LORENZO   I thank your honour. For my part, my lord,
My purpose was not to have seen you here,
But, meeting with Salerio by the way,
He did entreat me, past all saying nay,
To come with him along.

SALERIO   I did, my lord,   230
And I have reason for it. Signior Antonio
Commends him to you.   [*He gives Bassanio a letter.*

BASSANIO   Ere I ope his letter,
I pray you, tell me how my good friend doth.

SALERIO   Not sick, my lord, unless it be in mind;
Nor well, unless in mind: his letter there
Will show you his estate.   [*Bassanio opens the letter.*

GRATIANO   Nerissa, cheer yon stranger, bid her welcome.
Your hand, Salerio. What's the news from Venice?
How doth that royal merchant, good Antonio?
I know he will be glad of our success: 240

We are the Jasons, we have won the fleece!

SALERIO I would you had won the fleece that he hath lost.

PORTIA There are some shrewd contents in yon same paper,
That steals the colour from Bassanio's cheek;
Some dear friend dead, else nothing in the world
Could turn so much the constitution
Of any constant man. What, worse and worse?
With leave, Bassanio: I am half yourself,
And I must freely have the half of anything
That this same paper brings you.

BASSANIO   O sweet Portia,   250
Here are a few of the unpleasant'st words
That ever blotted paper. Gentle lady,
When I did first impart my love to you,
I freely told you all the wealth I had
Ran in my veins: I was a gentleman.
And then I told you true; and yet, dear lady,
Rating myself at nothing, you shall see
How much I was a braggart. When I told you
My state was nothing, I should then have told you
That I was worse than nothing; for, indeed,   260
I have engaged myself to a dear friend,
Engaged my friend to his mere enemy,
To feed my means. Here is a letter, lady,
The paper as the body of my friend,
And every word in it a gaping wound
Issuing life-blood. But is it true, Salerio?
Hath all his ventures failed? What, not one hit?
From Tripolis, from Mexico, and England,
From Lisbon, Barbary, and India,
And not one vessel scape the dreadful touch   270
Of merchant-marring rocks?

SALERIO   Not one, my lord.
Besides, it should appear that if he had
The present money to discharge the Jew,
He would not take it: never did I know
A creature that did bear the shape of man
So keen and greedy to confound a man.
He plies the Duke at morning and at night,

And doth impeach the freedom of the state
If they deny him justice. Twenty merchants,
The Duke himself, and the magnificoes   280
Of greatest port, have all persuaded with him,
But none can drive him from the envious plea
Of forfeiture, of justice, and his bond.

JESSICA   When I was with him, I have heard him swear
To Tubal and to Chus,[97] his countrymen,
That he would rather have Antonio's flesh
Than twenty times the value of the sum
That he did owe him; and I know, my lord,
If law, authority, and power deny not,
It will go hard with poor Antonio.   290

PORTIA   Is it your dear friend that is thus in trouble?

BASSANIO   The dearest friend to me, the kindest man,
The best-conditioned and unwearied spirit
In doing courtesies; and one in whom
The ancient Roman honour more appears
Than any that draws breath in Italy.

PORTIA   What sum owes he the Jew?

BASSANIO   For me, three thousand ducats.

PORTIA   What, no more?
Pay him six thousand, and deface the bond;
Double six thousand, and then treble that,   300
Before a friend of this description
Shall lose a hair thorough[98] Bassanio's fault.
First, go with me to church, and call me wife,
And then away to Venice to your friend:
For never shall you lie by Portia's side
With an unquiet soul! You shall have gold
To pay the petty debt twenty times over.
When it is paid, bring your true friend along.
My maid Nerissa and myself meantime
Will live as maids and widows. Come, away,   310
For you shall hence upon your wedding-day:
Bid your friends welcome, show a merry cheer;
Since you are dear bought, I will love you dear.
But let me hear the letter of your friend.

BASSANIO [*reads:*] 'Sweet Bassanio, my ships have all miscarried,
my creditors grow cruel, my estate is very low, my bond
to the Jew is forfeit; and since, in paying it, it is
impossible I should live, all debts are cleared between
you and I, if I might but see you at my death. Notwith-
standing, use your pleasure: if your love do not persuade   320
you to come, let not my letter.'

PORTIA   O love, dispatch all business, and be gone!

BASSANIO Since I have your good leave to go away,
I will make haste; but, till I come again,
No bed shall e'er be guilty of my stay,
Nor rest be interposer 'twixt us twain.

                                        [*Exeunt.*

SCENE 3.

A street in Venice.

Enter SHYLOCK, SOLANIO, ANTONIO *and a Jailor.*

SHYLOCK   Jailor, look to him; tell not me of mercy:
This is the fool that lent out money gratis.
Jailor, look to him.

ANTONIO   Hear me yet, good Shylock.

SHYLOCK   I'll have my bond; speak not against my bond;
I have sworn an oath that I will have my bond.
Thou call'dst me dog before thou hadst a cause,
But since I am a dog, beware my fangs.
The Duke shall grant me justice. I do wonder,
Thou naughty jailor, that thou art so fond
To come abroad with him at his request.

ANTONIO   I pray thee, hear me speak.   10

SHYLOCK   I'll have my bond. I will not hear thee speak.
I'll have my bond, and therefore speak no more.
I'll not be made a soft and dull-eyed fool,
To shake the head, relent, and sigh, and yield
To Christian intercessors. Follow not:
I'll have no speaking; I will have my bond.   [*Exit.*

SOLANIO   It is the most impenetrable cur

That ever kept with men.

ANTONIO   Let him alone.
I'll follow him no more with bootless prayers.   20
He seeks my life; his reason well I know:
I oft delivered from his forfeitures
Many that have at times made moan to me.
Therefore he hates me.

SOLANIO   I am sure the Duke
Will never grant this forfeiture to hold.

ANTONIO The Duke cannot deny the course of law:
For the commodity that strangers have
With us in Venice, if it be denied,
Will much impeach the justice of the state,
Since that the trade and profit of the city   30
Consisteth of all nations. Therefore, go.
These griefs and losses have so bated me,
That I shall hardly spare a pound of flesh
Tomorrow to my bloody creditor.
Well, jailor, on. Pray God, Bassanio come
To see me pay his debt, and then I care not.

                                                    [*Exeunt.*

SCENE 4.

Portia's house at Belmont.

Enter PORTIA, NERISSA, LORENZO, JESSICA, *and* BALTHAZAR.

LORENZO   Madam, although I speak it in your presence,
You have a noble and a true conceit
Of god-like amity, which appears most strongly
In bearing thus the absence of your lord.
But if you knew to whom you show this honour,
How true a gentleman you send relief,
How dear a lover of my lord your husband,
I know you would be prouder of the work
Than customary bounty can enforce you.

PORTIA   I never did repent for doing good,   10
Nor shall not now: for in companions
That do converse and waste the time together,
Whose souls do bear an egall yoke of love,⁹⁹
There must be needs a like proportion¹⁰⁰
Of lineaments, of manners, and of spirit;
Which makes me think that this Antonio,
Being the bosom lover of my lord,
Must needs be like my lord. If it be so,
How little is the cost I have bestowed
In purchasing the semblance of my soul   20
From out the state of hellish cruelty.
This comes too near the praising of myself,
Therefore no more of it: hear other things.
Lorenzo, I commit into your hands
The husbandry and manage of my house,
Until my lord's return. For mine own part,
I have toward heaven breathed a secret vow
To live in prayer and contemplation,
Only attended by Nerissa here,
Until her husband and my lord's return.   30
There is a monastery two miles off,
And there we will abide. I do desire you
Not to deny this imposition,

The which my love and some necessity
Now lays upon you.

LORENZO   Madam, with all my heart
I shall obey you in all fair commands.

PORTIA   My people do already know my mind,
And will acknowledge you and Jessica
In place of Lord Bassanio and myself.
So fare you well, till we shall meet again.   40

LORENZO Fair thoughts and happy hours attend on you!

JESSICA I wish your Ladyship all heart's content.

PORTIA   I thank you for your wish, and am well pleased
To wish it back on you: fare you well, Jessica.

                         [*Exeunt Jessica and Lorenzo.*

Now, Balthazar,
As I have ever found thee honest-true,
So let me find thee still. Take this same letter,
And use thou all th'endeavour of a man
In speed to Padua; see thou render this
Into my cousin's hands, Doctor Bellario;   50
And look what notes and garments he doth give thee,
Bring them, I pray thee, with imagined speed
Unto the traject, to the common ferry
Which trades to Venice. Waste no time in words,
But get thee gone. I shall be there before thee.

BALTHAZAR Madam, I go with all convenient speed.   [*Exit.*

PORTIA   Come on, Nerissa, I have work in hand
That you yet know not of; we'll see our husbands
Before they think of us!

NERISSA   Shall they see us?

PORTIA   They shall, Nerissa; but in such a habit,   60
That they shall think we are accomplishèd
With what we lack.[101] I'll hold thee any wager,
When we are both accoutered like young men,
I'll prove the prettier fellow of the two,
And wear my dagger with the braver grace,
And speak between the change of man and boy
With a reed-voice, and turn two mincing steps
Into a manly stride; and speak of frays
Like a fine bragging youth; and tell quaint lies,

How honourable ladies sought my love,   70
Which I denying, they fell sick and died –
I could not do withal![102] Then I'll repent,
And wish, for all that, that I had not killed them;
And twenty of these puny lies I'll tell,
That men shall swear I have discontinued school
Above a twelvemonth. I have within my mind
A thousand raw tricks of these bragging Jacks,
Which I will practise.

NERISSA   Why, shall we turn to men?

PORTIA   Fie, what a question's that,
If thou wert near a lewd interpreter![103]   80
But come, I'll tell thee all my whole device
When I am in my coach, which stays for us
At the park-gate; and therefore haste away,
For we must measure twenty miles today.

                                                    [*Exeunt.*

SCENE 5.

The garden of Portia's house.

Enter LANCELET *and* JESSICA.

LANCELET   Yes truly, for look you, the sins of the father are to be
laid upon the children;[104] therefore, I promise you, I
fear you. I was always plain with you, and so now I
speak my agitation of the matter: therefore, be o' good
cheer, for truly I think you are damned. There is but
one hope in it that can do you any good, and that is but
a kind of bastard hope neither.

JESSICA   And what hope is that, I pray thee?

LANCELET   Marry, you may partly hope that your father got you
not, that you are not the Jew's daughter.   10

JESSICA   That were a kind of bastard hope, indeed! So the sins
of my mother should be visited upon me.

LANCELET   Truly then, I fear you are damned both by father and
mother: thus when I shun Scylla, your father, I fall into
Charybdis,[105] your mother: well, you are gone both ways.

JESSICA   I shall be saved by my husband: he hath made me a Christian.[106]

LANCELET   Truly, the more to blame he. We were Christians enow before, e'en as many as could well live, one by another. This making of Christians will raise the price 20 of hogs: if we grow all to be pork-eaters, we shall not shortly have a rasher on the coals for money.

Enter LORENZO.

JESSICA   I'll tell my husband, Lancelet, what you say; here he comes.

LORENZO   I shall grow jealous of you shortly, Lancelet, if you thus get my wife into corners!

JESSICA   Nay, you need not fear us, Lorenzo. Lancelet and I are out.[107] He tells me flatly there's no mercy for me in heaven, because I am a Jew's daughter: and he says you are no good member of the commonwealth, for, in con- 30 verting Jews to Christians, you raise the price of pork.

LORENZO   [*to Lancelet:*] I shall answer that better to the common-wealth than you can the getting up of the negro's belly:[108] the Moor is with child by you, Lancelet!

LANCELET   It is much that the Moor should be more than reason: but if she be less than an honest woman, she is indeed more than I took her for.[109]

LORENZO   How every fool can play upon the word! I think the best grace of wit will shortly turn into silence, and discourse grow commendable in none only but parrots. Go in, 40 sirrah; bid them prepare for dinner.

LANCELET   That is done, sir; they have all stomachs.

LORENZO   Goodly Lord, what a wit-snapper are you! Then bid them prepare dinner.

LANCELET   That is done too, sir; only 'cover' is the word.

LORENZO   Will you cover then, sir?

LANCELET   Not so, sir, neither; I know my duty.[110]

LORENZO   Yet more quarrelling with occasion! Wilt thou show the whole wealth of thy wit in an instant? I pray thee, understand a plain man in his plain meaning: go to thy 50 fellows, bid them cover the table, serve in the meat, and we will come in to dinner.

LANCELET   For the table, sir, it shall be served in; for the meat, sir,
           it shall be covered; for your coming in to dinner, sir,
           why, let it be as humours and conceits shall govern.
                                                        [*Exit.*

LORENZO   O dear discretion, how his words are suited!
           The fool hath planted in his memory
           An army of good words, and I do know
           A many fools that stand in better place,
           Garnished like him, that for a tricksy word   60
           Defy the matter. How cheer'st thou, Jessica?[111]
           And now, good sweet, say thy opinion,
           How dost thou like the Lord Bassanio's wife?

JESSICA   Past all expressing. It is very meet
           The Lord Bassanio live an upright life,
           For, having such a blessing in his lady,
           He finds the joys of heaven here on earth;
           And if on earth he do not merit it,
           In reason he should never come to heaven!
           Why, if two gods should play some heavenly match,   70
           And on the wager lay two earthly women,
           And Portia one, there must be something else
           Pawned with the other, for the poor rude world
           Hath not her fellow.

LORENZO   Even such a husband
           Hast thou of me, as she is for a wife.

JESSICA   Nay, but ask my opinion too of that.

LORENZO   I will anon; first, let us go to dinner.

JESSICA   Nay, let me praise you while I have a stomach.

LORENZO   No, pray thee, let it serve for table-talk;
           Then, howsome'er thou speak'st, 'mong other things   80
           I shall digest it.

JESSICA   Well, I'll set you forth.
                                                      [*Exeunt.*

ACT 4, SCENE 1.

A Court of Justice.

Enter DUKE, *Magnificoes,* ANTONIO, BASSANIO, GRATIANO,
SALERIO, *officers, clerks and others.*

DUKE What, is Antonio here?
ANTONIO Ready, so please your grace.
DUKE I am sorry for thee; thou art come to answer
  A stony adversary, an inhuman wretch
  Uncapable of pity, void and empty
  From any dram of mercy.
ANTONIO   I have heard,
  Your grace hath ta'en great pains to qualify
  His rigorous course; but since he stands obdúrate,
  And that no lawful means can carry me
  Out of his envy's reach, I do oppose   10
  My patience to his fury, and am armed
  To suffer with a quietness of spirit
  The very tyranny and rage of his.
DUKE Go one, and call the Jew into the court.
SOLANIO He is ready at the door; he comes, my lord.

Enter SHYLOCK.

DUKE Make room, and let him stand before our face.
  Shylock, the world thinks, and I think so too,
  That thou but lead'st this fashion of thy malice
  To the last hour of act, and then 'tis thought
  Thou'lt show thy mercy and remorse more strange 20
  Than is thy strange[112] apparent cruelty;
  And where thou now exacts the penalty,
  Which is a pound of this poor merchant's flesh,
  Thou wilt not only loose the forfeiture,
  But, touched with human gentleness and love,
  Forgive a moiety of the principal,
  Glancing an eye of pity on his losses
  That have of late so huddled on his back:
  Enow to press a royal merchant down,

	And pluck commiseration of his state 30
	From brassy bosoms and rough hearts of flints,
	From stubborn Turks and Tartars never trained
	To offices of tender courtesy.
	We all expect a gentle answer, Jew.
SHYLOCK	I have possessed your grace of what I purpose,
	And by our holy Sabbath have I sworn
	To have the due and forfeit of my bond.
	If you deny it, let the danger light
	Upon your charter and your city's freedom.
	You'll ask me why I rather choose to have 40
	A weight of carrion flesh than to receive
	Three thousand ducats: I'll not answer that.
	But say it is my humour, is it answered?
	What if my house be troubled with a rat,
	And I be pleased to give ten thousand ducats
	To have it baned? What, are you answered yet?
	Some men there are love not a gaping pig,
	Some that are mad if they behold a cat,
	And others when the bagpipe sings i'th' nose
	Cannot contain their urine:[113] for affection 50
	Masters oft passion,[114] sways it to the mood
	Of what it likes or loathes. Now, for your answer:
	As there is no firm reason to be rendered,
	Why he cannot abide a gaping pig;
	Why he, a harmless necessary cat;
	Why he, a woollen bagpipe; but of force
	Must yield to such inevitable shame
	As to offend, himself being offended;
	So can I give no reason, nor I will not,
	More than a lodged hate and a certain loathing 60
	I bear Antonio, that I follow thus
	A losing suit against him. Are you answered?
BASSANIO	This is no answer, thou unfeeling man,
	To excuse the current of thy cruelty.
SHYLOCK	I am not bound to please thee with my answers.
BASSANIO	Do all men kill the things they do not love?
SHYLOCK	Hates any man the thing he would not kill?

BASSANIO	Every offence is not a hate at first.
SHYLOCK	What, wouldst thou have a serpent sting thee twice?
ANTONIO	I pray you, think you question with the Jew:[115] 70
	You may as well go stand upon the beach
	And bid the main flood bate his usual height;
	You may as well use question with the wolf
	Why he hath made the ewe bleat for the lamb;
	You may as well forbid the mountain pines
	To wag their high tops and to make no noise
	When they are fretten with the gusts of heaven;
	You may as well do any thing most hard,
	As seek to soften that – than which what's harder? –
	His Jewish heart. Therefore, I do beseech you, 80
	Make no moe offers, use no farther means,
	But with all brief and plain conveniency
	Let me have judgement, and the Jew his will.
BASSANIO	For thy three thousand ducats here is six.
SHYLOCK	If every ducat in six thousand ducats
	Were in six parts, and every part a ducat,
	I would not draw them: I would have my bond!
DUKE	How shalt thou hope for mercy, rend'ring none?
SHYLOCK	What judgement shall I dread, doing no wrong?
	You have among you many a purchased slave, 90
	Which, like your asses and your dogs and mules,
	You use in abject and in slavish parts,
	Because you bought them: shall I say to you,
	'Let them be free, marry them to your heirs.
	Why sweat they under burthens? Let their beds
	Be made as soft as yours, and let their palates
	Be seasoned with such viands'? You will answer,
	'The slaves are ours.' So do I answer you.
	The pound of flesh, which I demand of him,
	Is dearly bought, 'tis mine, and I will have it: 100
	If you deny me – fie upon your law! –
	There is no force in the decrees of Venice.
	I stand for judgement. Answer: shall I have it?
DUKE	Upon my power, I may dismiss this court,
	Unless Bellario, a learned doctor
	Whom I have sent for to determine this,

Come here today.

SALERIO   My lord, here stays without
A messenger with letters from the doctor,
New come from Padua.

DUKE   Bring us the letters; call the messenger.   [*Exit Salerio.* 110

BASSANIO   Good cheer, Antonio! What man, courage yet:
The Jew shall have my flesh, blood, bones, and all,
Ere thou shalt lose for me one drop of blood.

ANTONIO   I am a tainted wether of the flock,
Meetest for death. The weakest kind of fruit
Drops earliest to the ground, and so let me;
You cannot better be employed, Bassanio,
Than to live still, and write mine epitaph.

Enter SALERIO *with* NERISSA, *who is dressed as a lawyer's clerk.*

DUKE   Came you from Padua, from Bellario?

NERISSA   From both, my lord. Bellario greets your grace.   120
  [*She presents a letter. Meanwhile, Shylock whets his knife on his shoe.*

BASSANIO   Why dost thou whet thy knife so earnestly?

SHYLOCK   To cut the forfeiture from that bankrout there.

GRATIANO   Not on thy sole, but on thy soul, harsh Jew,
Thou mak'st thy knife keen; but no metal can,
No, not the hangman's axe, bear half the keenness
Of thy sharp envy: can no prayers pierce thee?

SHYLOCK   No, none that thou hast wit enough to make.

GRATIANO   O, be thou damned, inexecrable dog,
And for thy life let justice be accused![116]
Thou almost mak'st me waver in my faith,   130
To hold opinion with Pythagoras[117]
That souls of animals infuse themselves
Into the trunks of men: thy currish spirit
Governed a wolf, who, hanged for human slaughter,[118]
Even from the gallows did his fell soul fleet,
And, whilst thou layest in thy unhallowed dam,
Infused itself in thee; for thy desires
Are wolvish, bloody, starved, and ravenous.

SHYLOCK   Till thou canst rail the seal from off my bond,
Thou but offend'st thy lungs to speak so loud: 140
Repair thy wit, good youth, or it will fall

	To cureless ruin. I stand here for law.
DUKE	This letter from Bellario doth commend
	A young and learned doctor to our court:
	Where is he?
NERISSA	He attendeth here hard by
	To know your answer, whether you'll admit him.
DUKE	With all my heart: some three or four of you,
	Go give him courteous conduct to this place.

> [*Exeunt attendants.*

Meantime, the court shall hear Bellario's letter.
[*Reads:*] 'Your grace shall understand that at the receipt 150
of your letter I am very sick, but, in the instant that your
messenger came, in loving visitation was with me a
young doctor of Rome; his name is Balthazar.[119] I
acquainted him with the cause in controversy between
the Jew and Antonio the merchant: we turned o'er
many books together. He is furnished with my opinion,
which, bettered with his own learning (the greatness
whereof I cannot enough commend), comes with him
at my importunity to fill up your grace's request in my
stead. I beseech you, let his lack of years be no im- 160
pediment to let him lack a reverend estimation, for I
never knew so young a body with so old a head: I leave
him to your gracious acceptance, whose trial shall better
publish his commendation.'
You hear the learned Bellario, what he writes.

Enter attendants with PORTIA, *who is dressed as a lawyer.*

	And here, I take it, is the doctor come.
	Give me your hand. Come you from old Bellario?
PORTIA	I did, my lord.
DUKE	You are welcome. Take your place.
	Are you acquainted with the difference
	That holds this present question in the court? 170
PORTIA	I am informed thoroughly of the cause.[120]
	Which is the merchant here, and which the Jew?
DUKE	Antonio and old Shylock, both stand forth.
PORTIA	Is your name Shylock?
SHYLOCK	Shylock is my name.

PORTIA	Of a strange nature is the suit you follow,
	Yet in such rule that the Venetian law
	Cannot impugn you as you do proceed.
	[*To Antonio:*] You stand within his danger, do you not?
ANTONIO	Ay, so he says.
PORTIA	Do you confess the bond?
ANTONIO	I do.
PORTIA	Then must the Jew be merciful. 180
SHYLOCK	On what compulsion must I? Tell me that.
PORTIA	The quality of mercy is not strained:
	It droppeth as the gentle rain from heaven[121]
	Upon the place beneath. It is twice blessed:
	It blesseth him that gives, and him that takes.
	'Tis mightiest in the mightiest: it becomes
	The thronèd monarch better than his crown;
	His sceptre shows the force of temporal power,
	The attribute to awe and majesty,
	Wherein doth sit the dread and fear of kings; 190
	But mercy is above this sceptred sway.
	It is enthronèd in the hearts of kings;
	It is an attribute to God himself;
	And earthly power doth then show likest God's,
	When mercy seasons justice. Therefore, Jew,
	Though justice be thy plea, consider this,
	That in the course of justice none of us
	Should see salvation: we do pray for mercy,
	And that same prayer doth teach us all to render
	The deeds of mercy. I have spoke thus much, 200
	To mitigate the justice of thy plea,
	Which if thou follow, this strict court of Venice
	Must needs give sentence 'gainst the merchant there.
SHYLOCK	My deeds upon my head![122] I crave the law,
	The penalty and forfeit of my bond.
PORTIA	Is he not able to discharge the money?
BASSANIO	Yes, here I tender it for him in the court;
	Yea, twice the sum. If that will not suffice,
	I will be bound to pay it ten times o'er,
	On forfeit of my hands, my head, my heart. 210
	If this will not suffice, it must appear

	That malice bears down truth. And I beseech you,
	Wrest once the law to your authority:
	To do a great right, do a little wrong,
	And curb this cruel devil of his will.
PORTIA	It must not be; there is no power in Venice
	Can alter a decree establishèd:
	'Twill be recorded for a precedent,
	And many an error by the same example
	Will rush into the state. It cannot be.

That malice bears down truth. And I beseech you,
Wrest once the law to your authority:
To do a great right, do a little wrong,
And curb this cruel devil of his will.

PORTIA　It must not be; there is no power in Venice
Can alter a decree establishèd:
'Twill be recorded for a precedent,
And many an error by the same example
Will rush into the state. It cannot be.　　220

SHYLOCK　A Daniel come to judgement: yea, a Daniel![123]
O wise young judge, how I do honour thee!

PORTIA　I pray you, let me look upon the bond.

SHYLOCK　Here 'tis, most reverend doctor, here it is.

PORTIA　Shylock, there's thrice thy money offered thee.

SHYLOCK　An oath, an oath, I have an oath in heaven.
Shall I lay perjury upon my soul?
No, not for Venice.

PORTIA　　　　　　　　　　Why, this bond is forfeit,
And lawfully by this the Jew may claim
A pound of flesh, to be by him cut off　　230
Nearest the merchant's heart. Be merciful:
Take thrice thy money. Bid me tear the bond.

SHYLOCK　When it is paid, according to the tenour.
It doth appear you are a worthy judge,
You know the law, your exposition
Hath been most sound: I charge you by the law,
Whereof you are a well-deserving pillar,
Proceed to judgement: by my soul I swear,
There is no power in the tongue of man
To alter me. I stay here on my bond.　　240

ANTONIO　Most heartily I do beseech the court
To give the judgement.

PORTIA　　　　　　　　　　Why then, thus it is.
You must prepare your bosom for his knife —

SHYLOCK　O noble judge! O excellent young man!

PORTIA　— For the intent and purpose of the law
Hath full relation to the penalty,
Which here appeareth due upon the bond.

SHYLOCK　'Tis very true: O wise and upright judge!

	How much more elder art thou than thy looks!
PORTIA	Therefore, lay bare your bosom.
SHYLOCK	Ay, his breast. 250
	So says the bond, doth it not, noble judge?
	'Nearest his heart', those are the very words.
PORTIA	It is so. Are there balance here, to weigh
	The flesh?
SHYLOCK	I have them ready.
PORTIA	Have by some surgeon, Shylock, on your charge,
	To stop his wounds, lest he do bleed to death.
SHYLOCK	Is it so nominated in the bond?
PORTIA	It is not so expressed, but what of that?
	'Twere good you do so much for charity.
SHYLOCK	I cannot find it; 'tis not in the bond. 260
PORTIA	You merchant, have you anything to say?
ANTONIO	But little; I am armed and well prepared.
	Give me your hand, Bassanio, fare you well!
	Grieve not that I am fall'n to this for you;
	For herein Fortune shows herself more kind
	Than is her custom: it is still her use
	To let the wretched man outlive his wealth,
	To view with hollow eye and wrinkled brow
	An age of poverty; from which ling'ring penance
	Of such misery doth she cut me off. 270
	Commend me to your honourable wife,
	Tell her the process of Antonio's end,
	Say how I loved you, speak me fair in death;
	And when the tale is told, bid her be judge
	Whether Bassanio had not once a love.
	Repent but you that you shall lose your friend,
	And he repents not that he pays your debt:
	For if the Jew do cut but deep enough,
	I'll pay it instantly with all my heart.
BASSANIO	Antonio, I am married to a wife 280
	Which is as dear to me as life itself;
	But life itself, my wife, and all the world,
	Are not with me esteemed above thy life.
	I would lose all, ay, sacrifice them all
	Here to this devil, to deliver you.

PORTIA	Your wife would give you little thanks for that,
	If she were by to hear you make the offer.
GRATIANO	I have a wife whom, I protest, I love:
	I would she were in heaven, so she could
	Entreat some power to change this currish Jew. 290
NERISSA	'Tis well you offer it behind her back:
	The wish would make else an unquiet house.
SHYLOCK	These be the Christian husbands! I have a daughter –
	Would any of the stock of Bárrabas[124]
	Had been her husband, rather than a Christian!
	We trifle time, I pray thee pursue sentence.
PORTIA	A pound of that same merchant's flesh is thine:
	The court awards it, and the law doth give it.
SHYLOCK	Most rightful judge!
PORTIA	And you must cut this flesh from off his breast: 300
	The law allows it, and the court awards it.
SHYLOCK	Most learnèd judge! A sentence! Come, prepare.
PORTIA	Tarry a little; there is something else.
	This bond doth give thee here no jot of blood:
	The words expressly are 'a pound of flesh':
	Take then thy bond, take thou thy pound of flesh;
	But, in the cutting it, if thou dost shed
	One drop of Christian blood, thy lands and goods
	Are by the laws of Venice confiscate
	Unto the state of Venice. 310
GRATIANO	O upright judge! Mark, Jew. O learnèd judge!
SHYLOCK	Is that the law?
PORTIA	Thyself shalt see the act:
	For, as thou urgest justice, be assured
	Thou shalt have justice more than thou desir'st.
GRATIANO	O learnèd judge! Mark, Jew – a learnèd judge!
SHYLOCK	I take this offer then; pay the bond thrice,
	And let the Christian go.
BASSANIO	Here is the money.
PORTIA	Soft!
	The Jew shall have all justice; soft, no haste:
	He shall have nothing but the penalty. 320
GRATIANO	O Jew, an upright judge, a learnèd judge!
PORTIA	Therefore, prepare thee to cut off the flesh.

Shed thou no blood, nor cut thou less nor more
But just a pound of flesh. If thou tak'st more
Or less than a just pound, be it but so much
As makes it light or heavy in the substance,
Or the division of the twentieth part
Of one poor scruple – nay, if the scale do turn
But in the estimation of a hair –
Thou diest and all thy goods are confiscate.   330

GRATIANO A second Daniel, a Daniel, Jew!
Now, infidel, I have you on the hip.

PORTIA Why doth the Jew pause? Take thy forfeiture.

SHYLOCK Give me my principal, and let me go.

BASSANIO I have it ready for thee, here it is.

PORTIA He hath refused it in the open court;
He shall have merely justice and his bond.

GRATIANO A Daniel, still say I, a second Daniel!
I thank thee, Jew, for teaching me that word.

SHYLOCK Shall I not have barely my principal?   340

PORTIA Thou shalt have nothing but the forfeiture
To be so taken at thy peril, Jew.

SHYLOCK Why then, the devil give him good of it!
I'll stay no longer question.[125]

PORTIA   Tarry, Jew.
The law hath yet another hold on you.
It is enacted in the laws of Venice,
If it be proved against an alien
That by direct or indirect attempts
He seek the life of any citizen,
The party 'gainst the which he doth contrive   350
Shall seize one half his goods; the other half
Comes to the privy coffer of the state;
And the offender's life lies in the mercy
Of the Duke only, 'gainst all other voice.
In which predicament, I say, thou stand'st:
For it appears by manifest proceeding
That indirectly and directly too
Thou hast contrived against the very life
Of the defendant; and thou hast incurred
The danger formerly by me rehearsed.   360

	Down, therefore, and beg mercy of the Duke.
GRATIANO	Beg that thou mayst have leave to hang thyself.
	And yet, thy wealth being forfeit to the state,
	Thou hast not left the value of a cord;
	Therefore thou must be hanged at the state's charge.
DUKE	That thou shalt see the difference of our spirit,
	I pardon thee thy life before thou ask it.
	For half thy wealth, it is Antonio's;
	The other half comes to the general state,
	Which humbleness may drive unto a fine.

370

PORTIA	Ay, for the state, not for Antonio.
SHYLOCK	Nay, take my life and all, pardon not that.
	You take my house, when you do take the prop
	That doth sustain my house; you take my life,[126]
	When you do take the means whereby I live.
PORTIA	What mercy can you render him, Antonio?
GRATIANO	A halter gratis – nothing else, for God's sake.
ANTONIO	So please my lord the Duke and all the court
	To quit the fine for one half of his goods;
	I am content, so he will let me have

380

	The other half in use,[127] to render it
	Upon his death unto the gentleman
	That lately stole his daughter.
	Two things provided more: that, for this favour,
	He presently become a Christian;
	The other, that he do record a gift,
	Here in the court, of all he dies possessed,
	Unto his son Lorenzo and his daughter.
DUKE	He shall do this, or else I do recant
	The pardon that I late pronouncèd here.

390

PORTIA	Art thou contented, Jew? What dost thou say?
SHYLOCK	I am content.
PORTIA	[to Nerissa:] Clerk, draw a deed of gift.
SHYLOCK	I pray you give me leave to go from hence.
	I am not well. Send the deed after me,
	And I will sign it.
DUKE	Get thee gone, but do it.
GRATIANO	In christ'ning thou shalt have two godfathers;
	Had I been judge, thou shouldst have had ten more,

	To bring thee to the gallows, not the font.	
	[Exit Shylock.	
DUKE	*[to Portia:]* Sir, I entreat you home with me to dinner.	
PORTIA	I humbly do desire your grace of pardon:	400
	I must away this night toward Padua,	
	And it is meet I presently set forth.	
DUKE	I am sorry that your leisure serves you not.	
	Antonio, gratify this gentleman,	
	For in my mind you are much bound to him.	
	[Exeunt Duke, Magnificoes	
	and their train.	
BASSANIO	Most worthy gentleman, I and my friend	
	Have by your wisdom been this day acquitted	
	Of grievous penalties, in lieu whereof,	
	Three thousand ducats, due unto the Jew,	
	We freely cope your courteous pains withal.	410
ANTONIO	And stand indebted, over and above,	
	In love and service to you evermore.	
PORTIA	He is well paid that is well satisfied,	
	And I, delivering you, am satisfied,	
	And therein do account myself well paid.	
	My mind was never yet more mercenary.[128]	
	I pray you, know me when we meet again.	
	I wish you well, and so I take my leave.	
BASSANIO	Dear sir, of force I must attempt you further.	
	Take some remembrance of us, as a tribute,	420
	Not as a fee. Grant me two things, I pray you:	
	Not to deny me, and to pardon me.	
PORTIA	You press me far, and therefore I will yield.	
	Give me your gloves, I'll wear them for your sake.	
	And, for your love, I'll take this ring from you.	
	Do not draw back your hand: I'll take no more,	
	And you in love shall not deny me this!	
BASSANIO	This ring, good sir? Alas, it is a trifle;	
	I will not shame myself to give you this.	
PORTIA	I will have nothing else but only this;	430
	And now, methinks, I have a mind to it.	
BASSANIO	There's more depends on this than on the value.	
	The dearest ring in Venice will I give you,	

	And find it out by proclamation;
	Only for this, I pray you, pardon me.
PORTIA	I see, sir, you are liberal in offers.
	You taught me first to beg, and now, methinks,
	You teach me how a beggar should be answered.
BASSANIO	Good sir, this ring was given me by my wife;
	And when she put it on, she made me vow
	That I should neither sell, nor give, nor lose it.
PORTIA	That 'scuse serves many men to save their gifts;
	And if your wife be not a mad-woman,
	And know how well I have deserved this ring,
	She would not hold out enemy for ever
	For giving it to me. Well, peace be with you! [*Exeunt*
	Portia and Nerissa.
ANTONIO	My Lord Bassanio, let him have the ring.
	Let his deservings and my love withal
	Be valued 'gainst your wife's commandèment.[129]
BASSANIO	Go, Gratiano, run and overtake him,
	Give him the ring, and bring him if thou canst
	Unto Antonio's house. Away, make haste.
	[*Exit Gratiano.*
	Come, you and I will thither presently,
	And in the morning early will we both
	Fly toward Belmont. Come, Antonio.
	[*Exeunt.*

440

450

SCENE 2.

A street in Venice before the Court of Justice.

Enter PORTIA *and* NERISSA, *still disguised.*

PORTIA	Inquire the Jew's house out, give him this deed,
	And let him sign it. We'll away tonight,
	And be a day before our husbands home:
	This deed will be well welcome to Lorenzo.

Enter GRATIANO.

GRATIANO	Fair sir, you are well o'erta'en:

My Lord Bassanio, upon more advice,
Hath sent you here this ring, and doth entreat
Your company at dinner.

PORTIA   That cannot be.
His ring I do accept most thankfully,
And so, I pray you, tell him; furthermore,   10
I pray you, show my youth old Shylock's house.

GRATIANO That will I do.

NERISSA   Sir, I would speak with you.
[*Aside to Portia:*]
I'll see if I can get my husband's ring,
Which I did make him swear to keep for ever.

PORTIA [*aside to Nerissa:*]
Thou mayst, I warrant. We shall have old swearing
That they did give the rings away to men;
But we'll outface them, and outswear them too.
Away, make haste, thou know'st where I will tarry.
                                        [*Exit.*

NERISSA Come, good sir, will you show me to this house?
                                        [*Exeunt.*

ACT 5, SCENE 1.

The garden before Portia's house at Belmont.

Enter LORENZO *and* JESSICA.

LORENZO   The moon shines bright. In such a night as this,
When the sweet wind did gently kiss the trees
And they did make no noise, in such a night
Troilus methinks mounted the Troyan walls,
And sighed his soul toward the Grecian tents
Where Cressid lay that night.[130]

JESSICA   In such a night
Did Thisbe fearfully o'ertrip the dew,
And saw the lion's shadow ere himself,[131]
And ran dismayed away.[132]

LORENZO   In such a night
Stood Dido with a willow in her hand[133]   10
Upon the wild sea banks, and waft her love
To come again to Carthage.[134]

JESSICA   In such a night
Medea gathered the enchanted herbs
That did renew old Aeson.[135]

LORENZO   In such a night
Did Jessica steal from the wealthy Jew,
And with an unthrift love did run from Venice
As far as Belmont.

JESSICA   In such a night
Did young Lorenzo swear he loved her well,
Stealing her soul with many vows of faith,
And ne'er a true one.

LORENZO   In such a night   20
Did pretty Jessica (like a little shrew)
Slander her love, and he forgave it her.

JESSICA   I would out-night you, did no body come:
But, hark, I hear the footing of a man.

Enter STEPHANO.

LORENZO   Who comes so fast in silence of the night?

STEPHANO	A friend!
LORENZO	A friend – what friend? Your name, I pray you, friend?
STEPHANO	Stephano is my name, and I bring word

STEPHANO A friend!
LORENZO A friend – what friend? Your name, I pray you, friend?
STEPHANO Stephano is my name, and I bring word
My mistress will before the break of day
Be here at Belmont. She doth stray about   30
By holy crosses, where she kneels and prays
For happy wedlock hours.
LORENZO   Who comes with her?
STEPHANO None, but a holy hermit and her maid.
I pray you, is my master yet returned?
LORENZO He is not, nor we have not heard from him.
But go we in, I pray thee, Jessica,
And ceremoniously let us prepare
Some welcome for the mistress of the house.

Enter LANCELET.

LANCELET Sola, sola! Wo ha, ho, sola, sola![136]
LORENZO Who calls?   40
LANCELET Sola! Did you see Master Lorenzo? Master Lorenzo?
Sola, sola!
LORENZO Leave hollowing[137] man: here!
LANCELET Sola! Where, where?
LORENZO Here!
LANCELET Tell him, there's a post come from my master, with his
horn full of good news.[138] My master will be here ere
morning.   [*Exit.*
LORENZO Sweet soul, let's in, and there expect their coming.
And yet no matter: why should we go in?   50
My friend Stephano, signify, I pray you,
Within the house, your mistress is at hand,
And bring your music forth into the air.
                                    [*Exit Stephano.*
How sweet the moonlight sleeps upon this bank!
Here will we sit, and let the sounds of music
Creep in our ears: soft stillness and the night
Become the touches of sweet harmony.
Sit, Jessica. Look how the floor of heaven
Is thick inlaid with patens of bright gold.
There's not the smallest orb which thou behold'st 60
But in his motion like an angel sings,

Still quiring to the young-eyed cherubins.[139]
Such harmony is in immortal souls;
But whilst this muddy vesture of decay
Doth grossly close it in, we cannot hear it.[140]

Enter Musicians.

Come, ho, and wake Diana with a hymn![141]
With sweetest touches pierce your mistress' ear,
And draw her home with music.   [*Music begins.*

JESSICA   I am never merry when I hear sweet music.
LORENZO   The reason is, your spirits are attentive: 70
For do but note a wild and wanton herd,
Or race of youthful and unhandled colts,
Fetching mad bounds, bellowing and neighing loud,
Which is the hot condition of their blood;
If they but hear perchance a trumpet sound,
Or any air of music touch their ears,
You shall perceive them make a mutual stand,
Their savage eyes turned to a modest gaze
By the sweet power of music: therefore, the poet
Did feign that Orpheus drew trees, stones, and floods,[142] 80
Since nought so stockish, hard, and full of rage,
But music for the time doth change his nature.
The man that hath no music in himself,
Nor is not moved with concord of sweet sounds,
Is fit for treasons, stratagems, and spoils;
The motions of his spirit are dull as night,
And his affections dark as Erebus:[143]
Let no such man be trusted.[144] Mark the music.

Enter PORTIA *and* NERISSA.

PORTIA   That light we see is burning in my hall.
How far that little candle throws his beams![145]   90
So shines a good deed in a naughty world.
NERISSA   When the moon shone, we did not see the candle.
PORTIA   So doth the greater glory dim the less:
A substitute shines brightly as a king,
Until a king be by, and then his state
Empties itself, as doth an inland brook
Into the main of waters. Music, hark!

NERISSA   It is your music, madam, of the house.

PORTIA   Nothing is good, I see, without respect;[146]

    Methinks it sounds much sweeter than by day.   100

NERISSA   Silence bestows that virtue on it, madam.

PORTIA   The crow doth sing as sweetly as the lark

    When neither is attended; and I think

    The nightingale, if she should sing by day

    When every goose is cackling, would be thought

    No better a musician than the wren.

    How many things by season seasoned are

    To their right praise and true perfection.

    Peace, ho! [*The music ceases.*] The moon sleeps

                     with Endymion,

    And would not be awaked.[147]

LORENZO   That is the voice,   110

    Or I am much deceived, of Portia.

PORTIA   He knows me, as the blind man knows the cuckoo,

    By the bad voice.

LORENZO   Dear lady, welcome home!

PORTIA   We have been praying for our husbands' welfare,

    Which speed, we hope, the better for our words.

    Are they returned?

LORENZO   Madam, they are not yet;

    But there is come a messenger before,

    To signify their coming.

PORTIA   Go in, Nerissa,

    Give order to my servants that they take

    No note at all of our being absent hence;   120

    Nor you, Lorenzo; Jessica, nor you.

                             [*A tucket sounds.*

LORENZO   Your husband is at hand: I hear his trumpet.

    We are no tell-tales, madam; fear you not.

PORTIA   This night methinks is but the daylight sick;

    It looks a little paler; 'tis a day

    Such as the day is when the sun is hid.

    Enter BASSANIO, ANTONIO, GRATIANO *and their followers.*

BASSANIO   We should hold day with the Antipodes,

    If you would walk in absence of the sun.[148]

PORTIA   Let me give light, but let me not be light,

| | For a light wife doth make a heavy husband,[149] | 130 |

	For a light wife doth make a heavy husband,[149] 130
	And never be Bassanio so for me.
	But God sort all! You are welcome home, my lord.
	[Gratiano and Nerissa talk apart.
BASSANIO	I thank you, madam. Give welcome to my friend.
	This is the man, this is Antonio,
	To whom I am so infinitely bound.
PORTIA	You should in all sense be much bound to him,
	For, as I hear, he was much bound for you.[150]
ANTONIO	No more than I am well acquitted of.
PORTIA	Sir, you are very welcome to our house:
	It must appear in other ways than words, 140
	Therefore I scant this breathing courtesy.[151]
GRATIANO	*[to Nerissa:]* By yonder moon I swear you do me wrong.
	In faith, I gave it to the judge's clerk.
	Would he were gelt that had it, for my part,
	Since you do take it, love, so much at heart.
PORTIA	A quarrel, ho, already! What's the matter?
GRATIANO	About a hoop of gold, a paltry ring
	That she did give to me, whose posy was
	For all the world like cutler's poetry
	Upon a knife: 'Love me, and leave me not.'[152] 150
NERISSA	What talk you of the posy or the value?
	You swore to me when I did give it you
	That you would wear it till your hour of death,
	And that it should lie with you in your grave.
	Though not for me, yet for your vehement oaths,
	You should have been respective and have kept it.
	Gave it a judge's clerk! No, God's my judge,
	The clerk will ne'er wear hair on's face that had it.
GRATIANO	He will, an if he live to be a man.
NERISSA	Ay, if a woman live to be a man. 160
GRATIANO	Now, by this hand, I gave it to a youth,
	A kind of boy, a little scrubbèd boy,
	No higher than thyself, the judge's clerk,
	A prating boy, that begged it as a fee;
	I could not for my heart deny it him.
PORTIA	You were to blame – I must be plain with you –
	To part so slightly with your wife's first gift,

A thing stuck on with oaths upon your finger,
And so riveted with faith unto your flesh.
I gave my love a ring, and made him swear   170
Never to part with it, and here he stands:
I dare be sworn for him he would not leave it,
Nor pluck it from his finger, for the wealth
That the world masters. Now, in faith, Gratiano,
You give your wife too unkind cause of grief.
An 'twere to me, I should be mad at it.

BASSANIO [aside:] Why, I were best to cut my left hand off,
And swear I lost the ring defending it.

GRATIANO My Lord Bassanio gave his ring away
Unto the judge that begged it, and indeed   180
Deserved it too; and then the boy, his clerk,
That took some pains in writing, he begged mine,
And neither man nor master would take aught
But the two rings.

PORTIA [to Bassanio:]   What ring gave you, my lord?
Not that, I hope, which you received of me.

BASSANIO If I could add a lie unto a fault,
I would deny it; but you see my finger
Hath not the ring upon it: it is gone.

PORTIA Even so void is your false heart of truth.
By heaven, I will ne'er come in your bed   190
Until I see the ring!

NERISSA [to Gratiano:]   Nor I in yours,
Till I again see mine!

BASSANIO   Sweet Portia,
If you did know to whom I gave the ring,
If you did know for whom I gave the ring,
And would conceive for what I gave the ring,
And how unwillingly I left the ring,
When naught would be accepted but the ring,[153]
You would abate the strength of your displeasure.

PORTIA If you had known the virtue of the ring,
Or half her worthiness that gave the ring,   200
Or your own honour to contain the ring,
You would not then have parted with the ring.
What man is there so much unreasonable,

	If you had pleased to have defended it	
	With any terms of zeal, wanted the modesty	
	To urge the thing held as a ceremony?[154]	
	Nerissa teaches me what to believe:	
	I'll die for't but some woman had the ring!	
BASSANIO	No, by my honour, madam, by my soul,	
	No woman had it, but a civil doctor,	210
	Which did refuse three thousand ducats of me,	
	And begged the ring, the which I did deny him	
	And suffered him to go displeased away –	
	Even he that had held up the very life	
	Of my dear friend. What should I say, sweet lady?	
	I was enforced to send it after him.	
	I was beset with shame and courtesy:	
	My honour would not let ingratitude	
	So much besmear it. Pardon me, good lady,	
	For by these blessèd candles of the night,	220
	Had you been there, I think you would have begged	
	The ring of me to give the worthy doctor.	
PORTIA	Let not that doctor e'er come near my house.	
	Since he hath got the jewel that I loved,	
	And that which you did swear to keep for me,	
	I will become as liberal as you:	
	I'll not deny him any thing I have,	
	No, not my body, nor my husband's bed:	
	Know him I shall, I am well sure of it.	
	Lie not a night from home; watch me, like Argus:[155]	230
	If you do not, if I be left alone,	
	Now, by mine honour, which is yet mine own,	
	I'll have that doctor for my bedfellow.	
NERISSA	And I his clerk; therefore be well advised	
	How you do leave me to mine own protection.	
GRATIANO	Well, do you so: let not me take him then,	
	For if I do, I'll mar the young clerk's pen.[156]	
ANTONIO	I am th'unhappy subject of these quarrels.	
PORTIA	Sir, grieve not you; you are welcome notwithstanding.	
BASSANIO	Portia, forgive me this enforcèd wrong,	240
	And in the hearing of these many friends	
	I swear to thee, even by thine own fair eyes	

Wherein I see myself –

PORTIA   Mark you but that!
In both my eyes he doubly sees himself:
In each eye, one. Swear by your double self,
And there's an oath of credit.[157]

BASSANIO   Nay, but hear me.
Pardon this fault, and by my soul I swear
I never more will break an oath with thee.

ANTONIO I once did lend my body for his wealth,
Which but for him that had your husband's ring   250
Had quite miscarried.[158] I dare be bound again –
My soul upon the forfeit – that your lord
Will never more break faith advisedly.

PORTIA Then you shall be his surety.
[*She takes a ring from her finger.*] Give him this,
And bid him keep it better than the other.

ANTONIO Here, Lord Bassanio, swear to keep this ring.

BASSANIO By heaven, it is the same I gave the doctor!

PORTIA I had it of him: pardon me, Bassanio,
For by this ring the doctor lay with me.

NERISSA [*shows a ring also.*]
And pardon me, my gentle Gratiano,   260
For that same scrubbèd boy, the doctor's clerk,
In lieu of this last night did lie with me.

GRATIANO Why, this is like the mending of highways
In summer, where the ways are fair enough!
What, are we cuckolds ere we have deserved it?[159]

PORTIA Speak not so grossly. You are all amazed.
Here is a letter: read it at your leisure.
It comes from Padua, from Bellario;
There you shall find that Portia was the doctor,
Nerissa there, her clerk. Lorenzo here   270
Shall witness I set forth as soon as you,
And even but now returned; I have not yet
Entered my house. Antonio, you are welcome,
And I have better news in store for you
Than you expect: unseal this letter soon,
There you shall find three of your argosies
Are richly come to harbour suddenly.

           You shall not know by what strange accident
           I chancèd on this letter.

ANTONIO   I am dumb!

BASSANIO Were you the doctor, and I knew you not?   280

GRATIANO Were you the clerk that is to make me cuckold?

NERISSA Ay, but the clerk that never means to do it,
           Unless he live until he be a man.

BASSANIO Sweet doctor, you shall be my bedfellow:
           When I am absent, then lie with my wife.

ANTONIO Sweet lady, you have given me life and living;
           For here I read for certain that my ships
           Are safely come to road.

PORTIA   How now, Lorenzo?
           My clerk hath some good comforts too for you.

NERISSA Ay, and I'll give them him without a fee.   290
           There do I give to you and Jessica,
           From the rich Jew, a special deed of gift,
           After his death, of all he dies possessed of.

LORENZO Fair ladies, you drop manna in the way
           Of starvèd people.[160]

PORTIA   It is almost morning,
           And yet I am sure you are not satisfied
           Of these events at full. Let us go in,
           And charge us there upon inter'gatories,[161]
           And we will answer all things faithfully.

GRATIANO Let it be so. The first inter'gatory   300
           That my Nerissa shall be sworn on is,
           Whether till the next night she had rather stay,
           Or go to bed now, being two hours to day.
           But were the day come, I should wish it dark,
           Till I were couching with the doctor's clerk.
           Well, while I live, I'll fear no other thing
           So sore as keeping safe Nerissa's ring.[162]

                           [*Exeunt.*

NOTES ON *THE MERCHANT OF VENICE*

In these notes, the following abbreviations are used:

- *c.*   *circa* (approximately);
- cf.   *confer* (compare);
- F1   First Folio;
- i.e.   *id est* (that is);
- O.E.D.   *The Oxford English Dictionary* (London: Oxford University Press, 1933; rpt. 1961);
- Q1   First Quarto;
- S.D.   stage direction.

In the case of a pun or an ambiguity, the meanings are distinguished as (a) and (b).

1 (1.1.9) *argosies with portly sail:* 'large mercantile ships with swelling sails'.

2 (1.1.27) Andrew *docked in sand:* Andrew is the name of a sailing ship, perhaps suggested by the *San Andrés* (*St Andrew*) captured at Cádiz in 1596; and 'docked in sand' means 'stuck in a sand-bank'.

3 (1.1.28–9) *Vailing . . . burial:* 'lowering her topmast below the framework of the hull to kiss her grave'.

4 (1.1.84) *grandsire cut:* 'grandfather sculpted'.

5 (1.1.112) *In a neat's . . . vendible:* 'in cured ox-tongue (a delicacy) and in an unmarriagable woman'. (Furthermore, the phrase 'a dried neat's tongue' could refer bawdily to an impotent old man.)

6 (1.1.166) *Brutus' Portia:* Portia (the wife of Marcus Junius Brutus) is depicted in *Julius Caesar* as noble and devoted.

7 (1.1.170–2) *golden fleece . . . Colchos' strand . . . Jasons:* The legendary Jason and his Argonauts sailed to 'Colchos' (usually 'Colchis') to gain the Golden Fleece.

8 (1.2.7) *in the mean:* 'in the midpoint, avoiding extremes'.

9 (1.2.43–4) *An . . . choose!:* Perhaps 'If you will not accept me as a husband, please yourself!'.

10 (1.2.45–6) *weeping philosopher:* Heraclitus of Ephesus, *c.*500 BC, who was said to have wept at human folly.

11 (1.2.72) *neighbourly charity:* cf. 'Charitie worketh no ill to his neighbour' (Bishops' Bible: Romans 13:10).

12 (1.2.75–6) *became . . . another:* 'became his guarantor, and set his seal to the agreement'.

13 (1.2.99) *old as Sibylla:* According to Ovid's *Metamorphoses* (Bk. 14), Apollo granted the prophetess, the Cumaean Sibyl, as many years of life as there were grains in a heap of dust.

14 (1.2.99–100) *chaste as Diana:* Diana was the Roman goddess of chastity.

15 (1.2.121) *complexion of a devil:* Devils were often regarded as black-skinned.

16 (1.3.1) *Three thousand ducats:* a huge sum, worth at least ten times the £60 that Shakespeare paid for a large house in 1597.

17 (1.3.29–30) *the habitation . . . into:* Mark 4:1–20 tells that Jesus (who had lived in Nazareth) took the devil and devils known as Legion from a man and put them into a herd of swine which then rushed into the sea and drowned. Matthew 8:28–34 and Luke 8:26–39 give alternative versions. Traditionally, Jews do not eat pork: Leviticus 11:7 says that the pig is unclean.

18 (1.3.29–33) *Yes . . . with you:* Some editors treat this speech, from 'Yes, to smell pork' to 'pray with you.', as an aside.

19 (1.3.36) *fawning publican:* Luke 18:10–14 contrasts a penitent, humble 'publican' (tax-gatherer) with a proud Pharisee. 'Publican' could also mean 'inn-keeper'.

20 (1.3.52) *Tubal:* The original Tubal (Genesis 10:2) was a grandson of Noah.

21 (1.3.67–9) *This Jacob . . . third:* The 'first possessor' was Abraham, the second was Isaac, and the third should have been Esau; but Rebekah, Jacob's 'wise mother', disguised Jacob with animals' skins so that blind Isaac mistakenly transferred the inheritance to him instead of to the hairy Esau. See Genesis, Chap. 27.

22 (1.3.72–83) *mark . . . Jacob's:* Laban agreed that Jacob should be rewarded by being allocated the particoloured animals in Laban's

flocks. Jacob then outwitted him by placing particoloured rods in front of the animals, so that, when they bred, the offspring were similarly coloured; and thus a greater proportion became Jacob's. See Genesis, 30:31–43.

23 (1.3.93) *The devil . . . purpose:* proverbial, following Matthew 4:6 and Luke 4:10, in which Satan indeed quotes Scripture.

24 (1.3.128–9) *take . . . metal:* 'take increase from a loan of inanimate metal'. Antonio is using a traditional argument against usury: that it is unnatural, since metal cannot breed.

25 (1.3.140) *single bond:* formal agreement to pay a debt on a particular day.

26 (2.1.2) *The shadowed . . . sun:* 'the dark uniform (black skin-colour) issued by the resplendent sun'.

27 (2.1.8–9) *this aspect . . . valiant:* 'my appearance has frightened the brave'.

28 (2.1.25–6) *That slew . . . Solyman:* 'which slew the Emperor of Persia and a Persian prince who had won three battles against Suleiman, Sultan of the Turks'. (Suleiman 'the Magnificent' lived from *c.*1495 to 1566.)

29 (2.1.32) *Hercules and Lichas:* Lichas is a servant in the legend of Hercules; here Shakespeare gives his name to a temple-curator who played the god at dice.

30 (2.1.35) *So is Alcides . . . page:* Alcides is another name for Hercules. In this line, 'page' is a common emendation of 'rage', the noun that appears in Q1 and F1.

31 (2.2. S.D.) *Lancelet Gobbo:* Q1 and F1 variously spell the Christian name as 'Launcelet' and 'Lancelet' and the surname as 'Jobbe' and 'Gobbo'. 'Launcelet' or 'lancelet' could mean 'small knife (or lancet)'; 'gobbo' is Italian for 'hunchback'.

32 (2.2.24–5) *devil incarnation:* He means 'devil incarnate'.

33 (2.2.33) *sand-blind, high gravel-blind:* 'sand-blind' means 'partly blind'; 'high gravel-blind' (Lancelet's invention) means 'almost stone-blind (i.e. almost completely blind)'.

34 (2.2.58) *Sisters Three:* the three Fates, Clotho, Lachesis and Atropos, who allocated life and death.

35 (2.2.71–2) *a wise father . . . child:* a reversal of the proverb, 'It is a wise child that knows its own father'.

36 (2.2.88–9) *What . . . tail:* a comic analogy to Isaac's deception by the disguised Jacob.

37 (2.2.96–7) *set up my rest:*   a term from the card–game Primero, meaning 'staked all I have'.

38 (2.2.117) *infection:*   He muddles 'intention' and 'affection'.

39 (2.2.125) *frutify:*   He muddles 'fructify', 'certify' and 'notify'.

40 (2.2.128) *impertinent:*   He muddles 'importunate' and 'pertinent'.

41 (2.2.133) *defect:*   He means 'effect' or 'fact'.

42 (2.2.139) *The old proverb:*   The proverb is (with variants): 'He that hath the grace of God hath enough.'

43 (2.2.144–5) *a livery . . . guarded:*   'a uniform better ornamented'.

44 (2.2.148) *table:*   In palmistry, the 'table' is the quadrangular area formed by four main lines in the palm of the hand. Lancelet reads his own palm.

45 (2.2.150) *line of life:*   the curving line at the base of the thumb.

46 (2.2.156–7) *in the twinkling:*   of an eye.

47 (2.3.10) *exhibit:*   He means 'inhibit'.

48 (2.5.20) *reproach:*   He means 'approach', but Shylock takes it literally.

49 (2.5.22–6) *I will . . . afternoon:*   This nonsense mocks Shylock's superstitious fears.

50 (2.5.29) *wry-necked fife:*   'crooked-necked fife-player'.

51 (2.5.35) *Jacob's staff:*   Jacob set out as a poor man with his staff but returned wealthy (see Genesis 32:10 and Hebrews 11:21).

52 (2.5.42) *Jewess' eye:*   Q1 and F1 have 'Iewes eye'. Alexander Pope emended this to 'Jewess' eye' (meaning, of course, 'Jessica's recognition'). An alternative reading could be 'Jewè's eye', the sounded 'è' preserving the original metre. 'As dear as a Jew's eye' was proverbial, meaning 'As valuable to someone as is keen perception to a Jew'.

53 (2.5.43) *fool of Hagar's offspring:*   'buffoon suitable for (or de-scended from) Hagar's offspring'. Hagar was Abraham's concu-bine. She and her son, Ishmael, were sent into exile, and Ishmael became a hated pariah. (See Genesis 16 and 21:9–21).

54 (2.5.53) *'Fast . . . find':*   a proverb meaning 'If you secure things firmly, you will later find them quickly'.

55 (2.6. S.D.) *Salarino:*   This name appears here in Q1 as 'Salerino', in F1 as 'Salino'. Some editors change the name in this scene to Salerio. J. L. Halio, following M. M. Mahood, assumes that

Salarino does not exit with Jessica and Lorenzo and can therefore witness the parting of Bassanio from Antonio that he describes in Act 2 scene 8. But the text (at 2.6.60–68) strongly implies that Salarino, Jessica and Lorenzo have exited together; so the description of the parting may simply be a Shakespearian inconsistency.

56 (2.6.5) *Venus' pigeons:* Venus's flying chariot was hauled by doves.

57 (2.6.5–7) *ten . . . unforfeited!:* i.e.: 'Lovers are ten times swifter to enjoy copulation than they are to keep their promise to marry.'

58 (2.6.14) *younger:* Some editors emend the 'younger' of Q1 and 'yonger' of F1 to 'younker', meaning 'young nobleman'. But 'younger' (perhaps implying a son who, not being the heir, sets out to try to make his fortune) offers sufficient sense. (The biblical Prodigal Son was the younger son.)

59 (2.6.17) *How like . . . return:* The Prodigal Son returned impoverished (see Luke 15:11–32).

60 (2.6.42) *light:* (a) wanton, immodest; (b) glaring.

61 (2.6.43–4) *'tis . . . obscured:* 'the duty of a torch-bearer is to reveal, but I ought to remain concealed'.

62 (2.6.45) *lowly garnish:* 'humble outfit'. Most editors read as 'lovely' here the 'louely' of Q1 and F1. I follow Halio in treating 'lowly' as a more plausible reading in this context.

63 (2.6.47) *For . . . runaway:* 'because the secretive night is rapidly passing'.

64 (2.7.22) *silver . . . hue?:* The moon has a silvery light, and Diana, goddess of chastity, is the moon-goddess.

65 (2.7.51) *To rib . . . grave:* 'to enclose in the dark grave the waxed cloth (enfolding her corpse)'.

66 (2.7.56) *a coin . . . angel:* This gold coin bore the figure of the Archangel Michael.

67 (2.8.18) *sealèd bag, two sealèd:* Shakespeare usually treats 'seal' as a monosyllable; hence the accents here, to preserve the metre.

68 (2.9.61–2) *To offend . . . offices:* 'The criminal and the judge have different rôles and opposed natures' (i.e. 'Don't try to judge the justice of your failure').

69 (2.9.63) *fire:* pronounced disyllabically ('*fi*-er'), preserving the metre.

70 (2.9.64–5) *Seven . . . amiss:* cf. Psalms 12:6 (Geneva Bible): 'The wordes of the Lord *are* pure wordes: as the siluer, tried in a fornace of earth, fined [i.e. refined] seuen folde.'

71 (2.9.78) *wroth:* (a) 'wrath', anger; (b) 'ruth', sorrow. Q1 and F1 have 'wroath'.

72 (2.9.80–81) *O, these . . . lose:* 'Oh, these deliberating fools! When they choose, they are so excessively wise that, by means of their intelligence, they fail.' (Or: ' . . . When they choose, their intelligence leads them to failure – which, in my view, is tantamount to wisdom.')

73 (3.1.32) *Out . . . years?:* Solanio facetiously pretends that Shylock meant not 'My daughter to turn against me!' but 'My carnal appetites rebel against restraint!'.

74 (3.1.77–8) *The curse . . . now:* Editors suggest that 'the curse' may be: Jesus' condemnation of Jerusalem for a range of sins including the killing of prophets (Matthew 23:33–9; Luke 13:34–5); St Paul's declaration that God favours the gentiles rather than the Jews (Romans 9:30–31); and the blood-guilt accepted by Jews for condemning Jesus (Matthew 27:25). The last seems the most likely. In the Geneva Bible, the people say: 'His blood *be* on vs, and on our children'; and the marginal gloss adds: '[A]nd as they wished, so this cursse taketh place to this day.'

75 (3.1.96) *here in Genoa:* As Shylock is in Venice, some editors change the 'heere' of Q1 and 'here' of F1 to 'there' or 'heard'; but by 'here in Genoa' Shylock may mean 'in this land of Italy (where Genoa lies)'.

76 (3.1.108) *turquoise:* The turquoise would be an appropriate semi-precious stone for a betrothal ring, since it was said to remove enmity and reconcile man and wife.

77 (3.2.4) *but it is not love:* The phrasing may be corrupt, since she proceeds to make clear that it *is* love. ('What is it but love?' or 'but is it not love?' might fit.)

78 (3.2.8) *a maiden . . . thought:* 'a maiden should not say aloud what she thinks'.

79 (3.2.20) *Prove it so:* 'If it prove so' (i.e., if it should happen that she cannot be united with him).

80 (3.2.22) *peize:* Q1 and F1 have 'peize', which means 'hang weights on' (and thus 'draw out'). Some editors prefer the spelling 'peise' or the emendation 'piece' ('extend').

81 (3.2.25) *the rack:* This was a torture-machine which stretched victims, tearing their joints; sometimes 'confessions' were thus elicited.

82 (3.2.28–9) *that ugly . . . love:* cf. Troilus (in *Troilus and Cressida*, Act 3, scene 2), who fears that the sexual encounter will be like death or swooning, or will exceed his capacity: 'I fear it much'. Dover Wilson, however, reads 'fear' as 'doubt', so that 'fear th'enjoying of my love' may mean only 'doubt that I shall succeed in my courtship'.

83 (3.2.44) *swan-like end:* Swans were supposed to sing as they died.

84 (3.2.55–60) *young Alcides . . . exploit:* Ovid's *Metamorphoses* says that Hercules (Alcides) rescued the Trojan princess, Hesione, who had been chained to rocks as a sacrifice to Neptune, the sea-god. He did so to win a reward of horses, not Hesione herself. Thus Bassanio strives with 'much more love'. ('Dardanian' means 'Trojan'.)

85 (S.D. following 3.2.62) *before:* Q1's stage direction is '*A Song the whilst Bassanio comments on the caskets to himselfe*'. I change '*the whilst*' to '*before*', because his opening comment, 'So may the outward shows be least themselves', is clearly the moral that he has aptly elicited from the song.

86 (3.2.63) *Fancy:* aesthetic attraction as opposed to true love.

87 (3.2.63–65) *bred . . . head . . . nourishèd:* The rhyme-syllable rhymes with 'lead', and thus may give a hint to Bassanio. Furthermore, the song helpfully warns him against being fooled by appearances. At 1.2.88–91 Portia had thought of influencing (adversely) another suitor's choice.

88 (3.2.87–8) *And these . . . redoubted:* 'And such people need only put on the outward appearance of valour in order to be deemed redoubtable.' ('Excrement' means literally 'outgrowth', e.g. the beard.)

89 (3.2.89) *by the weight:* fair hair was bought by weight to make wigs.

90 (3.2.91) *lightest:* The adjective punningly brings to mind 'lightest in weight' but means (a) brightest, fairest, and (b) most immodest.

91 (3.2.101) *Then:* Q1 and F1 have 'Therefore then'. My emendation restores the pentameter.

92 (3.2.102) *Hard food for Midas:*   King Midas wished that all he touched would turn to gold, but repented this wish when his food was thus transformed.

93 (3.2.132) *Chance . . . true:*   Perhaps '(who) hazard becomingly and choose truly'.

94 (3.2.159) *sum of something:*   Q1 has 'sume of something'; F1 has 'sum of nothing'. J. Dover Wilson reads 'some of something'. Here, 'sum of something' means 'merely the whole of some thing'.

95 (3.2.192) *none from me:*   'none from me in addition to the complete joy that you will have wished each other'.

96 (3.2.214–17) *We'll . . . down:*   Gratiano says: 'We'll have a bet: the first couple to produce a boy will win a thousand ducats.' Nerissa replies: 'What! Do we have to put stakes down (place our bets) already?' Gratiano says: 'We'll never win at the game (the gamble or the sexual game) if our stakes are down (i.e. if our penises are dangling limply).'

97 (3.2.285) *Chus:*   The original Chus was the eldest son of Ham and the father of Nimrod (Genesis 10:6–9). 'Chus' is the spelling in the Bishops' Bible, 'Cush' the spelling in the Geneva Bible.

98 (3.2.302) *thorough:*   Q1 and F1 have 'through', but this word was often pronounced disyllabically (approximating 'thor-*roo*', the intended pronunciation here), making the line metrically regular.

99 (3.4.13) *an egall yoke of love:*   'a symmetrically-balanced attachment of love'. (Q1's 'egall' is a version of 'equal'.)

100 (3.4.14) *There must . . . proportion:*   'There must necessarily be a corresponding symmetry'.

101 (3.4.61–2) *accomplishèd . . . lack:*   i.e. equipped with male genitalia.

102 (3.4.72) *I could not do withal!:*   (a) 'I couldn't help it!'; (b) 'I really couldn't bring myself to copulate with them!'

103 (3.4.80) *a lewd interpreter!:*   i.e., one who would interpret her question not as 'Are we going to turn ourselves into men?' but as 'Are we going to make ourselves sexually available to men?'.

104 (3.5.1–2) *the sins . . . children:*   Exodus 20:5 (Geneva Bible): 'I am the Lord thy God, a ielouse God, visiting the iniquitie of the fathers vpon the children . . . '. Cf. Exodus 34:7; Deuteronomy 5:9; the Book of Common Prayer; and the Catechism.

105 (3.5.14–15) *Scylla . . . Charybdis:*   In Homer's *Odyssey*, Book
12, Odysseus's ship sails perilously between Scylla (a monster)
and Charybdis (a whirlpool). (Lancelet's 'fall into . . . your
mother' has an obvious bawdy sense.)

106 (3.5.16–17) *I . . . Christian:*   1 Corinthians 7:14 says that the
unbelieving wife is sanctified by the husband.

107 (3.5.27–8) *are out:*   (a) 'are in the open'; (b) 'are quarrelling'.

108 (3.5.34) *getting up . . . belly:*   'making the Negress pregnant'.

109 (3.5.36–7) *if she . . . for:*   (a) 'if she be no honest woman but a
promiscuous one, she is indeed more than I thought (and
sexually has had more experience than with me)'; (b) 'if the
worst you can say of her is that she is "less than honest", she is
actually better than I had assumed'.

110 (3.5.45–7) *only 'cover' . . . duty:*   Lancelet says that the correct
term is not 'prepare dinner' but 'cover' ('lay the table'); and,
when Lorenzo accordingly asks him to 'cover', Lancelet wilfully
takes that to mean 'put your hat on, instead of doffing it as a
sign of respect'.

111 (3.5.60–61) *Garnished . . . Jessica?:*   'similarly equipped with wit
(or similarly dressed in livery), who, for the sake of clever word-
play, flout the substantial sense. How are you feeling, Jessica?'

112 (4.1.20–21) *strange . . . strange:*   The first strange means 'remarkable', the second (probably) 'abnormal'.

113 (4.1.49–50) *others . . . urine:*   Contemporaneous writers (Zachary
Jones in *A Treatise of Spectres* and Ben Jonson in *Every Man in His
Humour*) made similar allegations of the diuretic effect of bagpipes.

114 (4.1.50–51) *for affection / Masters oft passion:*   (Perhaps) 'for
instinct often governs emotion'. Q1 has 'for affection. /
Maisters of passion'; F1 has 'for affection. / Masters oft passion'.
Editorial conjectures include: 'for affection, / Master of passion'
and 'for affection, / Mistress of passion'.

115 (4.1.70) *I pray . . . Jew:*   'I ask you – you who think you are
debating with the Jew – to consider this'.

116 (4.1.129) *And for . . . accused!:*   'and let it be regarded as a
miscarriage of justice that you were ever born!' (or 'that you
have never been sentenced to death!').

117 (4.1.131) *Pythagoras:*   philosopher and mathematician (*c.*540 BC)
who propounded the doctrine of the transmigration of souls
(metempsychosis).

118 (4.1.134) *wolf . . . slaughter:* Usurers were often likened to wolves, and predatory animals were occasionally tried and hanged. Some editors speculate that this passage may refer to the hanging in 1594 of Dr Roderigo (or Ruy) López, a Portuguese of Jewish descent, who was a physician to Queen Elizabeth. (Q1 spells 'wolf ' here with a capital W; and the name 'López' resembles 'lupus', Latin for 'wolf'.) The trial of López was characterised by anti-Semitic fervour, and thus forms a significant part of the background to *The Merchant of Venice*. Nevertheless, the speculation, though ingenious, does not fit well the context here. Shylock must have lain 'in his unhallowed dam' long before the date of López's death.

119 (4.1.153) *Balthazar:* The name derives from 'Belteshazzar', the Chaldean name of the prophet Daniel (see Book of Daniel, Chap. 4).

120 (4.1.171) *I . . . cause:* 'Throughly' (in Q1 and F1) was probably pronounced trisyllabically ('thor-*roo*-ly'), making the line a regular iambic pentameter. Hence my emendation, 'thoroughly'.

121 (4.1.182–3) *The quality . . . heaven:* cf. Ecclesiasticus 35:19 (Geneva Bible): 'Oh, how faire a thing is mercie in the time of anguish and trouble! It is like a cloude of raine, that cometh in the time of a drought.'

122 (4.1.204) *My deeds . . . head!:* Perhaps another echo of Matthew 27:25, which reports that the Jewish people, when insisting on the crucifixion of Christ, declared their readiness to accept the blood-guilt.

123 (4.1.221) *A Daniel . . . Daniel!:* In Hebrew, the name 'Daniel' means 'The Judge of the Lord'. In 'The Historie of Susanna' (Apocrypha, Geneva Bible), he is the very young judge ('a yong childe') who, perceiving that the two elders are falsely accusing Susanna, uses their own evidence to convict them.

124 (4.1.294) *Bárrabas:* the murderer whom the people of Jerusalem freed while demanding the death of Jesus (and the name of the hero-villain of Marlowe's *The Jew of Malta*).

125 (4.1.344) *I'll . . . question:* 'I'll remain here no longer to argue the case.'

126 (4.1.374) *you take my life:* cf. Ecclesiasticus 34:23 (Geneva Bible): 'He that taketh away his neighbour[']s liuing, slayeth him . . . '

127 (4.1.381) *in use:*   Antonio says he is willing that the state should take nothing from Shylock, provided that he himself can use half Shylock's wealth. 'In use' can mean 'for purposes of usury'; but that would be out of character, given that Antonio has hitherto lent money gratis. 'In trust for business purposes' is a suitably vague gloss.

128 (4.1.416) *My mind . . . mercenary:*   'In my career, I have never sought more than my clients' satisfaction.'

129 (4.1.449) *commandèment:*   Q1 has 'commaundement', F1 'commandement'. Both indicate quadrisyllabic pronunciation, which makes the line regular.

130 (5.1.4–6) *Troilus . . . night:*   Shakespeare's *Troilus and Cressida* will tell how Trojan Troilus lost his love, Cressida, when she was obliged to return with her father to the Greeks and subsequently proved unfaithful to him. (Chaucer's *Troilus and Criseyde*, Bk. 5, describes Troilus addressing the moon and walking the moonlit battlements as he pines for Criseyde.)

131 (5.1.8) *shadow ere himself:*   'shadow (or reflection) before she saw the lion himself'.

132 (5.1.7–9) *Did Thisbe . . . away:*   Thisbe arranged to meet her lover, Pyramus, at night in the woods. There she was frightened by a lion (or lioness) with bloodstained jaws, and ran away. The lion tore the veil which she had left behind. Pyramus, finding the bloodstained veil, assumed that Thisbe had been killed, and therefore committed suicide. Thisbe emerged, found him dying, and slew herself. Shakespeare could have found this story in Ovid's *Metamorphoses* and in Chaucer's *Legend of Good Women*. He parodies it in *A Midsummer Night's Dream*, and its plot-culmination resembles the ending of *Romeo and Juliet*.

133 (5.1.10) *a willow in her hand:*   a willow wand or sprig, the willow being an emblem of forsaken love.

134 (5.1.9–12) *In such . . . Carthage:*   Dido, Queen of Carthage, was loved but then deserted by Aeneas, who sailed away across the Mediterranean; so, distraught, she killed herself. (Shakespeare would have known various versions, found in, for example, Virgil's *Aeneid*, Ovid's *Heroides* and *Metamorphoses*, Chaucer's *Legend of Good Women* and Marlowe's *Dido, Queen of Carthage*.)

135 (5.1.12–14) *In such . . . Aeson:*   Medea, the legendary enchantress, indeed gathered herbs for a brew which she used as a

transfusion to replace Aeson's blood and rejuvenate him. (Aeson's son, Jason, was loved by Medea, but he deserted her and their children.) Sources include Ovid's *Metamorphoses* and Chaucer's *Legend of Good Women*.

136 (5.1.39) *Sola . . . sola!:*   He imitates the sound of a post-horn.

137 (5.1.43) *hollowing:*   Both Q1 and F1 have 'hollowing', meaning 'hallooing' or (to give a modern colloquial counterpart) 'hollering'.

138 (5.1.46–7) *his . . . news:*   Lancelet treats the post-horn as a cornucopia (horn of plenty).

139 (5.1.62) *young-eyed cherubins:*   The cherubins or cherubim, angels in the second rank of the ninefold hierarchy of heaven, were supposed to be vigilantly sharp-sighted.

140 (5.1.60–65) *There's not . . . hear it:*   Lorenzo cites the ancient notion that the stars and planets are set in crystalline spheres which make celestial music as they rotate, though humans are unable to hear it. (Sources include Plato's *Republic*, Plutarch's *De Musica* and Montaigne's *Essais*.)

141 (5.1.66) *wake . . . hymn!:*   Diana is the goddess of the moon and of chastity; so the command may be to play so well as (a) to draw the moon from behind a cloud, or (b) to hurry home the virgin-bride Portia, or (c) to do both.

142 (5.1.79–80) *the poet . . . floods:*   Ovid's *Metamorphoses* (Bks. 10 and 11) says that Orpheus' music attracted woods and rocks.

143 (5.1.87) *Erebus:*   in classical mythology, the utterly dark cavernous region through which the shades of the dead travelled to Hades.

144 (5.1.83–8) *The man . . . trusted:*   cf. Shylock in Act 2, scene 5, and Cassius in *Julius Caesar*, Act 1, scene 2.

145 (5.1.90) *How far . . . beams!:*   cf. Matthew 5:15–16 (Geneva Bible): 'Nether do men light a candel, and put it vnder a bushel, but on a candelsticke, & it giueth light vnto all that are in the house. Let your light so shine before men, that they may se[e] your good workes, & glorifie your Father which is in heauen.'

146 (5.1.99) *without respect:*   without relationship to a context.

147 (5.1.109–10) *The moon . . . awaked:*   Endymion was a young shepherd whom Selene (the moon-goddess of Greek mythology) visited each night as he, in a cave, slept an eternal sleep (perhaps induced by the goddess). Portia may be referring (a) to the fact

that the moon is now obscured, or (b) to the sight of Jessica in
Lorenzo's arms, or (c) to both.

148 (5.1.127–8) *We should . . . sun:* 'If you walked about when the
sun was absent, your presence would brighten our side of the
world, so that we should enjoy as much daylight then as do
people on the opposite side of the world (who, when it is night
for us, experience day).'

149 (5.1.129–30) *Let me . . . husband:* Using the rhetorical
procedure known as 'antanaclasis', she exploits the following
ambiguities. 'Light' can mean 'illumination', 'promiscuous' and
'light in weight'; 'heavy' can mean 'heavy in weight' and
'melancholy'.

150 (5.1.134–7) *This is . . . for you:* Here, 'bound' means variously
'held in bonds of friendship', 'obliged, indebted', 'pledged' and
'held prisoner'; while 'in all sense' means both 'for every reason'
and 'in the full sense of the word'.

151 (5.1.141) *scant . . . courtesy:* 'cut short these compliments in
words'.

152 (5.1.148–50) *whose posy . . . not':* A 'posy' is the motto
engraved on the inside of a ring. Cutlers engraved mottoes on
knives.

153 (5.1.193–7) *If you . . . ring:* His ostentatious rhetoric includes
the figures 'parison' (parallel structure), 'isocolon' (equal lengths)
and 'epistrophe' (ending two or more phrases or clauses with
the same word). Portia parodies the rhetoric.

154 (5.1.205–6) *wanted . . . ceremony?:* (probably:) 'that he would
inconsiderately press his demand for the item you retained as a
symbol?'

155 (5.1.230) *watch . . . Argus:* Argus Panoptes (the All-Seeing) was
a giant with a hundred eyes. At the command of Zeus's consort,
Hera, he guarded Io, a maiden transformed into a heifer; but
Hermes slew him, and Zeus eventually succeeded in copulating
with Io.

156 (5.1.237) *pen:* (a) quill-pen; (b) penis.

157 (5.1.245–6) *Swear . . . credit:* 'Swear doubly (therefore
duplicitously, like a double-crosser), and that's a believable and
trustworthy oath – I don't think!'

158 (5.1.249–51) *I once . . . miscarried:* The statement makes clear
that the interchangeability of living bodies and inanimate

symbols of value (bonds, rings) is a theme linking the different levels of the plot.

159 (5.1.263–5) *this is . . . deserved it?:* 'This is excessive, like mending roads in summer before winter has had an opportunity to damage them; for you, our wives, have made us cuckolds before we have had an opportunity to be unfaithful to you!'

160 (5.1.294–5) *you drop . . . people:* Exodus, Chap. 16, says that when Moses and the Israelites were hungry in the wilderness, God supplied them with manna, a form of bread. (Shylock might deem this allusion cruelly ironic.)

161 (5.1.298) *charge . . . inter'gatories:* 'compel us (like witnesses speaking under oath) to respond to interrogation'.

162 (5.1.307) *Nerissa's ring:* (a) the ring she gave him; (b) her vulva.

GLOSSARY

Where a pun or an ambiguity is intended, the meanings are distinguished as (a) and (b). Otherwise, alternative meanings are distinguished as (i) and (ii). Abbreviations include the following: O.E.D., *Oxford English Dictionary*; S.D., Stage Direction; vb., verb.

a (pronoun): he (2.1.30).

abode: delay (2.6.21).

Abram: Abraham, the first of the biblical patriarchs and progenitor of the Hebrew people.

acquitted of: rewarded for (5.1.138).

address: prepare.

advice: consideration (4.2.6).

advise: consider, reflect.

affection: disposition, instinct.

again: in consequence (3.2.204).

amazed: bewildered.

an: if.

angel: gold coin depicting the archangel Michael.

an't: if it.

appropriation: special attribute.

approve: justify (3.2.79).

argosy: very large mercantile ship.

aspect: appearance.

assume: take formally (2.9.51).

attentive: observant.

baned: poisoned.

bankrout: bankrupt.

bate: reduce.

best-conditioned: best-tempered.

betimes: quickly, soon.

Black Monday: Easter Monday.

blunt: (a) simple and direct; (b) lumpen, dull.

bondman: serf, slave.

bootless: fruitless.

bottom: ship (1.1.42).

break: fail (1.3.131).

break up: unseal a letter (2.4.10).

candle: **hold a candle to**: (a) illuminate; (b) stand by and observe.

carrion: (i) putrefying (4.1.41); (ii) fleshless (2.7.63); (iii, noun:) skeleton (3.1.32).

cater-cousins, scarce: hardly close friends.

cerecloth: winding-sheet (literally, cloth impregnated with wax).

ceremony: symbol (5.1.206).

cheer: face (3.2.312).

cherubim: clear-sighted high-ranking angels.

choir (vb.): make music.

choose!: please yourself! (1.2.44).

circumstance: circumlocution (1.1.154).

cold: finished, dead (2.7.73).

colt: 'young or inexperienced person' (*O.E.D.*).

coming-in: (a) allowance; (b) sexual gratification (2.2.152).

commodity: (i) goods; (ii) advantage, privileges.

complexion: disposition, nature.

compromised, to be: to be in agreement about an arrangement.

condition: character (1.2.120).

constant: steady, consistent.

contain: retain.

continent: contents, gist.

cope: pay for (4.1.410).

County (from Italian 'conte'): Count.

cover: (a) lay the table; (b) cover the head (3.5.45-7).

crisped: curled.

danger, within his: at his mercy, in his power.

Dardanian: Trojan.

Death: death's-head, skull (2.7.63).

dimensions: bodily parts or proportions (3.1.53).

disable: disparage.

discharge: pay (a debt).

discover: reveal (e.g. by drawing aside a curtain).

discretion: discrimination.

doit: coin or sum of very low value.

doublet: close-fitting jacket.

ducat: Spanish gold coin (the 'double ducat' being a coin of twice the value).

dull: blunt.

dumb-show: mimed part of a play.

eaning time: time of giving birth.

eanling: new-born lamb.

egall: equal.

eke: extend.

election: selection, choice.

Erebus: darkest region of the classical underworld.

ergo (Latin): therefore.

even: impartial (2.7.25).

excrement: outgrowth of the body: e.g. beard (3.2.87).

exeunt (Latin): they go out.

exit (Latin): he or she goes out.

Fancy: inclination, aesthetic attraction.

favour: leniency (4.1.384).

feared: frightened (2.1.9).

fia: mispronunciation of 'via' (Italian for 'away').

fill-horse: cart-horse.

find forth: find out, locate.

fledge: obsolete form of 'fledged'.

flight, of the self-same: of identical characteristics.

flourish (noun, S.D.): trumpet fanfare.

fond: foolish (2.9.27, 3.3.9).

fore-spurrer: swift horse-borne herald.

fulsome: (perhaps) lustful (*O.E.D.*).

gaberdine: long loose coat or cloak.

gaged: pledged.

gaping pig: roasted pig, open-mouthed, as served at a banquet.

garnish: outfit, costume.

garnished: (a) equipped with words; (b) dressed (3.5.60).

gear: purpose, business.

gelt: gelded, castrated.

gentle: (a) well-mannered; (b) Gentile (2.4.34).

glean: pick, remove.

gondylo: gondola.

Goodwins: Goodwin Sands, in the English Channel off the Kentish coast.

gossip: older woman who enjoys idle talk.

gramercy: thank you (literally, 'God grant you mercy').

grandam: grandmother.

gravel-blind: jocular link between 'sand-blind' (partly- or half-blind) and 'stone-blind' (completely blind).

groat: coin of very low value.

grow to: (a) incline towards; (b, possibly) lust after; (c, possibly) become tumescent (2.2.16).

guarded: ornamented (2.2.145).

gudgeon: small fish deemed gullible and easily-caught.

guilèd: wily, treacherous.

halter: rope with noose.

hearsèd: coffined.

heavens, for the: in heaven's name.

high-day: holiday.

hip: to catch or have upon the hip: to take at a disadvantage.

hollowing: hallooing, hollering.

hood, by my: a common oath, perhaps meaning 'by my state in life', though here Gratiano may be referring to a hood he is wearing (2.6.51).

humility: sufferance (sarcastic at 3.1.62).

husbandry: housekeeping.

Hyrcania: land south of the Caspian Sea, proverbial for wildness and savagery.

imagined speed: speed equal to that of the imagination.

impeach: discredit, call in question.

imposition: stipulation.

impugn: controvert, dispute.

incarnation: (garbled version of) incarnate.

incision, make: cut to draw blood.

inexecrable: (perhaps an intensive of 'execrable':) that cannot be sufficiently cursed.

infection: (muddle of) intention and affection (2.2.117).

insculped upon: with the design superimposed.

inter'gatory: legal interrogation on oath.

intermission: delay, relinquishment (3.2.200).

iwis: certainly.

Jack: lad; young rascal.

Janus: two-faced Roman god of thresholds.

jump with: agree with.

knap: munch.

leave: part with, lose (5.1.150, 172, 196).

level at: aim at, concentrate on.

Lichas: servant of Hercules.

lieu: payment, reward, acknowledgement.

light: (a) wanton, immodest; (b) bright (2.6.42).

likely: (a) likeable, attractive; (b) appropriate (2.9.92).

livery: uniform or insignia of an important person's servants.

look what: whatever (3.4.51).

magnifico: Venetian grandee.

mantle (vb.): become scum-covered.

mark: God bless the mark: an apologetic phrase used when something unpleasant or offensive is mentioned.

mart: market, exchange.

match (noun): bargain (3.1.39).

mere: sheer.

mind of love: love-scheme.

misconstered: misconstrued.

moe: more in number. ('Moe' was formerly differentiated from 'more', meaning 'greater in quantity').

moiety: share, portion (literally half).

mortifying: (i) penitential; (ii) death-causing, fatal. (Sighs and groans were supposed to drain blood from the heart.)

motions: impulses (5.1.86).

mutual: combined; shared by two or more.

naughty: wicked, bad.

neat's tongue: cured or dried ox-tongue.

needs, be: be necessarily.

Nestor: wise old leader of the Greeks at the siege of Troy.

obligèd faith: solemn promise (e.g. to marry).

occasion, with: (perhaps) opportunistic (3.5.48).

offence: annoyance.

officer: bailiff.

old (colloquial): ample (4.2.15).

opinion: reputation.

ostent: show, display.

o'er-look: bewitch by means of an 'evil eye' (3.2.15).

overpeer: look down on.

over-weathered: weather-beaten.

pageant: (i) movable scaffold (float) for plays and displays; (ii) decorated barge in an aquatic display.

parcel: batch.

part (vb.): depart (2.7.77).

patch (noun): fool.

paten: small metal dish used in the Mass.

pawn: stake, wager.

peevish: morose.

peize: draw out, prolong.

pent-house: overhanging roof or projecting structure.

pill (vb.): peel, strip.

port: life-style (1.1.124).

posy: inscribed motto.

presently: immediately.

prest unto: (i) ready for; (ii) compelled to.

prevent: forestall, anticipate.

prize, in a: in a match, for a prize.

publican: (i, probably:) tax-collector; (ii, possibly:) innkeeper.

purchase: acquire, gain (2.9.43).

quaint: skilful, cunning.

qualify: moderate, temper.

quality: (i) manner, style; (ii) trait, characteristic.

quiring: singing together like choristers.

race: herd or stud (5.1.72).

rack (vb.): stretch.

rate (noun): (i) style, mode of living (1.1.127); (ii) rate of interest (1.3.99).

rate (vb.): (i) berate (1.3.102); (ii) value (2.7.26).

reason (vb.): talk, converse (2.8.27).

rebel (vb.): lust.

reed-voice: squeaking voice.

regreets: salutations.

rehearse: cite, repeat.

respect, without: without reference to other things (5.1.99).

respective: careful, conscientious.

rest, set up one's: (a) gamble everything; (b) be resolved.

Rhenish: white wine from the Rhine region.

Rialto, the: (i) the Exchange at Venice, where merchants met; (ii) the Rialto Bridge (Ponte di Rialto), near the Exchange.

rib (vb.): enclose.

rightly: (i) correctly; (ii) truly.

road: roadstead (1.1.19).

ruin: rubbish, detritus (2.9.48).

sad: (i) serious (2.2.184); (ii) melancholy.

sand-blind: half-blind or partly-blind.

scant (vb.): restrict, cut short.

scape (noun): escapade.

scape (vb.): escape.

scarfèd: decked with streamers.

scimitar: curved sword.

scrubbèd: undersized, insignificant.

scruple: very small weight (20 grains in the apothecary's measure, amounting to just over one gramme).

season (vb.): alleviate, temper.

sense, in all: (a) for every reason; (b) in the full sense (5.1.136).

sensible: tangible.

sentences: maxims (1.2.10).

servitor: attendant.

set forth: (a) extol; (b) serve at table (3.5.81).

set up one's rest: (a) gamble everything; (b) be resolved.

shadowed: shaded, darkened.

shrine: (a) sacred place containing the remains of a saint; (b) enshrined image of a saint.

shrive: hear a confession and give absolution.

Sibylla: the Cumaean Sibyl, who was granted innumerable years of life.

simple (used ironically): unremarkable, humble (2.2.150, 152).

single bond: pledge to pay a sum by a specified date.

Sisters Three: the classical Fates (Clotho, Lachesis and

Atropos), who allotted the span of each person's life.

slips of prolixity: lapses into longwindedness.

slubber: perform in a hasty, slovenly manner.

smack: (a) savour of (lechery); (b, possibly) kiss (2.2.15).

smug: sprucely (3.1.41).

Soft!: Wait!

sonties: (probably) saints.

soon at: towards, near.

sooth: truth.

Sophy: a title of the Shah of Persia.

sort (noun): method (1.2.97).

sort (vb.): ordain, arrange (5.1.132).

sped: (a) finished; (b) hastened away (2.9.72).

spet: spit.

spirits: faculties of perception (*O.E.D.*; 5.1.70).

sufficient: financially sound (1.3.14–15, 23).

Sultan Solyman: Suleiman 'the Magnificent', Sultan of Turkey.

supposition, in: uncertain, doubtful.

table. In palmistry, the 'table' is the quadrangular area formed by four main lines in the palm of the hand.

terms: respect (2.1.13).

thrift: (i) thriving, success (1.1.175); (ii) gain, profit (1.3.45, 85).

time: time of life: here, youth (1.1.129).

touches: notes (5.1.57).

traject (from Italian 'traghetto'): ferry.

tried: assayed (2.7.53).

troth: faith, truth. **By my troth**: truly.

tucket: flourish on a trumpet.

turn to: sexually attract (1.3.76); at 3.4.78–80, (a) turn into, (b) sexually invite.

tyranny: cruelty (4.1.13).

umbered: shadowed, darkened.

unbated: anabated.

unhandled: not broken in.

untread: retrace.

usance: usury, interest.

vail: lower.

vantage: opportunity.

vendible: salable at the 'marriage-market' (1.1.112).

venture (noun): commercial speculation (1.1.15, 21, 42; 1.3.18).

very: true (2.2.98).

void rheum: spit.

warranty: authorisation.

well to live: in good health.

will (noun): (i) desire; (ii) testament.

wind about: approach circuitously.

wings, woven: sails.

wit-snapper: wisecracker, punmonger.

wrack: wreck.

wroth: (a) wrath, anger; (b) ruth, pity.

wry-necked fife: crooked-necked fife-player.